DONALD G. PATERSON is a member of the department of Economics at the University of British Columbia.

Some seventy years ago, at its peak, British investment in Canada accounted for over 20 per cent of British annual capital exports, and in the twenty-five years before World War I, for about 70 per cent of the capital flowing into Canada.

This study separates direct from portfolio investment (the form British investment has been assumed to prefer) and, on the basis of an analysis of the records of a thousand British companies active in the country, develops figures for UK direct investment in Canada from 1890 to 1914. It also suggests reasons for the decline of investment after the war: British firms found themselves at a disadvantage because there was little devolution of management to Canada and because few subsidiary companies were formed.

British Direct Investment in Canada, 1890–1914 fills an important gap in our historical statistics and also opens a significant field in Canadian economic history. It should also prove interesting to students of British imperialism and capitalism.

D.G. PATERSON

British Direct Investment in Canada, 1890-1914

UNIVERSITY OF TORONTO PRESS
Toronto and Buffalo

Toronto and Buffalo
Printed in Canada

Library of Congress Cataloging in Publication Data

Paterson, D G
British direct investment in Canada, 1890-1914.
Bibliography: p.
1. Investments, British - Canada - History. I. Title.
HG5152.P33 332.6'7341'071 76-22429
ISBN 0-8020-5354-8

Contents

Acknowledgments

The assistance of many institutions and persons helped make this study possible. I would like to acknowledge the generous financial aid of the Canada Council and the Social Science Research Council of Canada. My own university financed much of the associated typing expenses and this debt is also noted. During the research phase of this study many courtesies were extended to me. In particular I would like to mention the cheerful co-operation of the staffs of the Public Record Office, the Companies Registration Office, and the Office of the Registrar of Companies in Scotland. The company registration bodies of the governments of Nova Scotia, Quebec, Manitoba, Alberta, and British Columbia all provided me with invaluable aid. With good grace, many librarians have tolerated unusual requests for research material; none were more obliging than those in the British Museum.

To my friend Barry Supple I extend my warm thanks. More than any other person he influenced the direction of this study and taught me much. Long discussions (often in pubs) with Kevin Burley, Ian Drummond, and Jack Madden helped shape this inquiry. Valuable critical comments and insights were offered by my colleagues. Among those who acted beyond the call of duty were Chris Archibald, Lou Cain, Knick Harley, John Helliwell, and Jim Rae, as well as the anonymous referees for the University of Toronto Press. R.I.K. Davidson shepherded the manuscript through various stages and in the course of his editorship we have become friends. Mrs G. Stevenson was responsible for the copy editing.

This book has been published with the help of a grant from the Social Science Research Council of Canada, using funds provided by the Canada Council, and a grant from the Publications Fund of the University of Toronto Press.

University of British Columbia D.G. PATERSON

Tables

Preface

Early investigations into what is now termed foreign direct investment tended to concentrate on that investment in the manufacturing sector. Generally, this was referred to as 'branch plant' investment. The phrase stemmed from the practice of external manufacturing companies establishing unincorporated factory branches. However, soon after World War I it was recognized by economists that investment by foreign businesses needed to be more precisely defined and the analysis needed to account for the large amount of this type of investment in the non-manufacturing sectors. In the 1920s the phrase 'foreign direct investment' came to acquire its present usage. I use the phrase 'British direct investment' to refer both to the flow of new funds and to the firm undertaking the business activity. This study uses the present-day definition of foreign direct investment in the historical context of British business activity in Canada in the late nineteenth and early twentieth centuries. Its prime objects are to quantify British direct investment in Canada and analyse its determinants.

Forcing a precise economic concept on an historical situation inevitably involves some awkwardness. This applies not only to the definition of the problem but also to the subsequent presentation of the evidence. Before the determinants of British direct investment in Canada for the 1890-1914 period could be analysed it was necessary to construct statistical estimates of this investment. Because of the complete absence of any historical data or estimates and because of the consequent critical nature of the estimates presented here, Chapter 1 attempts to clarify the exact procedure used in their construction. First, some definitions are provided and the survey method used as a basis for determining direct investments is outlined. A detailed account of the method of examining direct investments and defining sectors is given. Next, the limits of the coverage are defined. The statistical procedure used to construct the estimates is described along with some discussion of probable biases implicit in these estimates. Lastly, probable sources of error are examined and the steps taken to minimize such errors are indicated.

The study is organized in sections which present the main statistical material. Yearly new investment figures are presented and discussed separately from those on the stock of investment or dividends. Since more emphasis is placed on certain aspects of these estimates of British direct investment in Canada, some chapters are inordinately long while others are short by comparison. Also, the statistical material is presented in a variety of ways. For instance, yearly new investment is completely presented in the tables. On the other hand, the level of investment is only presented for selected years in tabular form in the appendices. Most of the data presented are given in dollars. The major tables are converted to Canadian dollars at £1 = $4.85.

Each chapter is subdivided into sections which present and discuss various sectors of the Canadian economy or certain characteristics of this investment within a specific topic. The use of these subdivisions, I hope, eases the digestion of some of the longer chapters. They are also used to distinguish between the various sectors so that the reader can more readily link the themes on, say, British direct investment in the utilities sector. A certain amount of repetition is also necessary to provide an easier transition from one theme to the next.

I have used the expedient of referring to the Prairie provinces by their post-1905 status. Both Alberta and Saskatchewan joined Confederation in 1905 as new provinces. Previously they had been part of the North West Territories. This avoids any confusion with the post-1905 North West Territories. It also serves to indicate which of the provincial governments was considered by the federal government to be the appropriate registering body when the company files of the then North West Territories were allocated to the respective provinces.

BRITISH DIRECT INVESTMENT IN CANADA, 1890-1914

1

Introduction

No single issue in contemporary Canada has been the subject of such prolonged debate as foreign direct investment yet usually without reference to the 'historical fact.' This neglect betrays two serious gaps in Canadian economic history. First, there is a lack of quantitative information and, second, few attempts have been made to examine the growth of foreign direct investment in order to isolate reasons for its early appearance in Canada. In this study new quantitative evidence is presented documenting the history of British direct investment in Canada. Such investment has roots that lie deep in Canada's colonial past and some of the early British enterprises so permeate Canadian history that they assume a Canadian identity. Yet, despite the early British business links, by the end of World War I the United States was the preeminent source of foreign direct investment in Canada. Consequently, this investigation documents the failure of British enterprise to persist as a major force in the Canadian economy.

The importance of the overall capital imports into Canada in the late nineteenth and early twentieth centuries lay in their sheer volume. One of the principal capital movements in the pre-1914 international economy, the capital imports, supplemented domestic savings and contributed to a period of growth unparallelled in Canada's experience. Throughout the twenty-five years prior to 1914 approximately 70 per cent of this flow originated in Great Britain.[1] The relationship between Canada and Great Britain was a symmetrical one.

1 K.A.H. Buckley, *Capital formation in Canada, 1896–1930* (Toronto, 1955), pp. 11, 66, 103. The ratio of net domestic capital formation to net domestic product was 10.1 for the period 1896–1905 and 14.8 for the period 1905–15. Net of capital imports, the ratios of net national capital formation to net national product stood at 5.5 and 2.7 for the same periods.

Canada was one of the major host areas of British capital exports and in some years absorbed as much as 22.6 per cent of all the overseas issues placed in Great Britain.[2] A relative decline in the proportion of capital exports to Australia, South Africa, and the United States accompanied the advent of Canada as the principal source for British capital exports after 1904.[3] This switch in the composition of British capital exports was accompanied by a fundamental change in the position of the United States to a net capital exporter for most years after 1897.[4] Thus, the Canadian capital imports from Great Britain in the immediate pre-1914 period took place within a different framework from that which had existed for most of the nineteenth century.

The capital inflow to Canada from Great Britain has long been the subject of economic inquiry. Jacob Viner first examined it in the context of the classical economic price-specie flow mechanism.[5] Viner's work inspired long debates on the nature of the transfer process and how purchasing power was transferred internationally in the Canadian case. Work by G. Meier[6] on the 'transfer problem' and by J.C. Ingram[7] on the balance of payments related this capital movement to Canadian economic growth and the expansion of Canadian exports rather than to simple price movements induced by the transfer of capital. As Viner's strict classical position became less tenable, the emphasis of economic inquiry tended to centre on the smoothness of the capital transfer, the growth of demand for capital in Canada, and the contribution of the supply of financial capital to economic growth in this period.[8] The massive quantity of capital imports in relation to domestic investment has made the subject one of the prime areas for the investigation of the impact of international capital movements.

2 M. Simon, 'New British investments in Canada, 1865–1914,' *Canadian Journal of Economics*, 3, no. 2 (1970), 241
3 A.K. Cairncross, *Home and foreign investment, 1870–1913* (Cambridge, 1953), p. 182
4 J.G. Williamson, *American growth and the balance of payments, 1820–1913* (Durham, N.C., 1964), pp. 255-8
5 J. Viner, *Canada's balance of international indebtedness, 1900–1913* (Cambridge, Mass., 1924)
6 G.M. Meier, 'Economic development and the transfer mechanism in Canada,' *Canadian Journal of Economics and Political Science*, 19, no. 1 (1953), 1–19
7 J.C. Ingram, 'Growth and capacity in Canada's balance of payments,' *American Economic Review*, 117, no. 1 (1957), 93-194
8 For example: Buckley (1955) and J.A. Stovel, *Canada in the world economy* (Cambridge, Mass., 1959), as well as Meier

Early investigations of this capital movement relied, for the most part, on the evidence of contemporary observers. In recent years balance of payments estimates have also been formulated. Although some of these estimates will be mentioned in more detail later, it is sufficient at present to note that they have seldom made distinctions among the elements that comprise the long-term capital account of the balance of payments. They have been either of the aggregate long-term capital import into Canada (which cannot be disaggregated) or of elements that roughly fall into the category of long-term portfolio capital imports.[9]

A distinction between portfolio and direct investment is critical to the study of Canada's capital imports because they are fundamentally different types of capital movements. Portfolio foreign investment is a contractual obligation, usually initiated within the host country, whereas foreign direct investment is usually initiated in the capital exporter and is an act of business enterprise. Because of the preponderance of portfolio capital imports into Canada from Great Britain, and because of the inappropriate nature of the overall estimates of the capital imports, the exact extent and nature of British direct investment in Canada has remained obscure. The ratio of portfolio to direct investment, usually assumed to be high, has never been given precisely. Investigation into British direct investment in Canada in the pre-1914 period has also been overshadowed by the extent of American participation in Canadian manufacturing[10] and by overall United States direct investment which has predominated since statistical registers have been kept (the late 1920s in Canada).[11]

The aims of this study are twofold: (a) to attempt to quantify British direct investment in Canada in the twenty-five years prior to World War I, and (b) to analyse the characteristics of this form of investment and the business enterprises involved. While the aims of the study are to some extent independent, together they provide a fuller understanding of this particular case of direct investment. It

9 See later in this chapter.

10 *The Monetary Times* 9 May 1919, 18–24. Field reckoned the extent of this investment to be $264.9 million (in terms of equity capital) in 388 manufacturing plants alone.

11 *British and Foreign Direct Investments in Canada and Canadian Direct Investments Abroad, 1936* Department of Trade and Commerce (Ottawa, 1938), 21, noted that 'British direct investment in Canada is of older establishment than American, but has been outdistanced in the twentieth century, especially in the post war years.'

will be possible to determine whether British direct investment was an important source of financial capital for the growing Canadian economy and if it was efficiently supplied. The flows of non-capital resources, such as entrepreneurship, can be gauged as well. The pattern and timing of British direct investment, which in turn influenced the extent of investment, are analysed to provide a comparison with British portfolio investment in Canada in this period. Because British direct investment by 1918 was not growing as quickly as American direct investment, it is necessary to inquire whether its characteristics were responsible for the retardation.

HISTORICAL ESTIMATES

The year 1890 was a significant one in the economic history of both Great Britain and Canada. It was the beginning of the decade during which the dampened economic activity of the previous two decades came to an end in both countries. British capital exports again began to expand[12] and in Canada the economy began to show signs of vigorous economic growth which was to last until the beginning of World War I. Specifically, 1890 marks the peak of both the Canadian (actually late 1889) and the British business cycles.[13] The coincident peaks dictate a logical starting point for the study of direct investment between Britain and Canada. The period 1890–1914 also encompasses the last long-swing (Kuznets cycle) of world economic activity which determined British net capital exports – a relationship characteristic of the pre-1914 international economy.[14]

'Before 1914 the concept of direct investment (in its present-day sense) was not clearly distinguished in the statistics from other (non-controlling) equity investment in private foreign enterprises.'[15] Nor, it may be added, was any distinction made when a British enterprise undertook exclusively foreign operations. If a British company was

12 M. Simon, 'The pattern of new British portfolio foreign investments 1865–1914,' in *Capital movements and economic development*, ed. J.H. Alder (London, 1967), p. 45

13 E.J. Chambers, 'Late nineteenth century business cycles in Canada,' *Canadian Journal of Economics and Political Science*, 30, no. 3 (1964), 406; A.F. Burns and W.C. Mitchell, *Measuring business cycles* (New York, 1946), p. 512

14 Williamson, pp. 189–216

15 A.I. Bloomfield, *Patterns of fluctuation in international investment before 1914*, Princeton Studies in International Finance No. 21 (Princeton, 1968), p. 4

obviously involved in foreign investment, such as a rubber plantation or an Argentinian cattle ranch, it was classified, by contemporary observers, as such. If, on the other hand, a new British company was not immediately identified from its name or known intentions as operating overseas, it was usually overlooked as a foreign investment. Thus, there is a danger that private British investment has been assessed too conservatively. Foreign private investment is divided into two parts. Where no control is exercised by residents of the capital exporter the equities are properly classified as private portfolio foreign investment, and where control is exercised the equities are considered to be a measure of direct foreign investment. British direct investment in Canada has been assumed to have been more modest than proper accounting might reveal.

The first of the contemporary estimates to throw light on the position of British direct investment in Canada prior to 1914 were supplied by Sir George Paish. In attempting to estimate the distribution of all British capital exports, he concluded that between 1907 and 1914 new British private investment in Canada approached 20 per cent of total new British investment.[16] This would be approximately $243 million, a high absolute figure for Canada. Paish's estimates, presented in various editions of the *Statist*, were made simply by observing the issues floated in the London capital market. His keen knowledge of the market produced global estimates which were surprisingly accurate.[17]

For this early period the estimates which give the clearest picture of British direct investment in Canada are those of F.W. Field. Field (editor of the major Canadian financial journal of the day, *The Monetary Times*) also constructed his estimates by direct observation of new company formation and new equity issues of existing companies. Field was not only a very careful observer of business activity in Canada but maintained intimate connections with the Skinners and the *Statist* newspaper. The Skinners edited and published several important business directories such as the *Stock Exchange Year Book* as well as the *Canadian Gazette*, a weekly newspaper published in London reporting exclusively on Canadian investment opportunities. By careful observation Field classified each issue and produced esti-

16 Viner (1924), p. 126

17 For a short discussion on how Paish's British net capital export estimates were amended by Feis and checked by Imlah see: B. Thomas, 'The Historical Record of International Capital Movements to 1913,' *Capital movements*, pp. 3-7.

TABLE 1.1
Miscellaneous British investments in Canada, 1905-13 (Field's estimates)

Sector	$ 000's 1905-9	1905-11	1905-13
Branch plants	—	—	6,000
Investments with loan and mortgage companies	5,720	8,725	12,000
Industrial investment	22,500	26,375	29,000
Mining investment	56,313	57,555	59,000
Land and lumber purchases	19,000	34,000	40,000
Urban property	—	8,525	25,000
Total	103,535	135,180	171,000

SOURCE: F.W. Field, *Capital Investments in Canada* (Toronto, 1914), 9

mates of British private investment in Canada. Then by subtracting the large investments in railways and a few other large companies where no British control was evident he arrived at estimates which he called 'miscellaneous British investments.' Since these estimates exclude much of what is now called equity portfolio investment, they are a close approximation of British direct investment in Canada. These have remained since 1914 the best estimates of this investment available.

Estimates made of the total inflow of British capital have also thrown some light on the direct investment component. The two most notable estimates are by Viner and Hartland.[18] Viner's estimates cover the period from 1900 to 1913, while Hartland's figures cover the earlier period from 1868 to 1899 (to coincide with Viner's series). Both authors relied on balance of payments data. For 1900 to 1913 Viner used Field's figures on private British investment, presented in Table 1.1, as a guideline (although he added $32.5 million for the investment of British life, fire and general insurance companies).[19] Hartland, unlike Viner, made some direct observations of the long-term direct (and private) capital imports into Canada for the period prior to 1900 (Table 1.2). She calculated that from 1868 to 1899 new British direct investment in Canada averaged about $3 million per year.

18 Viner (1924) and P. Hartland, 'The Canadian balance of payments since 1868,' *Trends in the American economy in the nineteenth century*, Studies in Income and Wealth. Vol. 24. NBER (Princeton, 1960), pp. 717-55

19 Viner (1924), p. 125

TABLE 1.2
The composition of foreign investment in Canada, 1868–1900
(Hartland's estimates)

	$ m	% of total	% of total excl. issues (%)
	(1)	(2)	(3)
Public issues	789	71.5	—
US direct and private investments	191	17.5	60.5
UK direct and private investments	90	8.0	28.5
Investments of all other countries	35	3.0	11.0
	1105	100.0	100.0

SOURCE: Hartland, 'Balance,' 740

Viner's yearly series for the period 1900–13 reveal the total British foreign investment in Canada, but Hartland's figures present only an aggregate for the period. However, in recent years the work of Professor M. Simon has solved part of this problem. Simon catalogued each new bond and equity issue placed by foreigners on the British Stock Exchanges (he also included the equity issues of British companies clearly operating abroad). By computing all new Canadian issues he was able to estimate, fairly closely, segments of the long-term capital inflow to Canada from Britain. Unfortunately, Simon's estimates, presented in Table 1.3, do not correspond exactly to portfolio investment because they include some elements of direct investment. As a result Simon's series may overstate slightly the amount of new British portfolio investment in Canada, but they are probably the most accurate figures on long-term British portfolio investment in Canada.[20] Throughout this study Simon's figures will be used to proxy new British portfolio investment.

Simon characterized British 'portfolio' investment in Canada in the pre-1914 period as essentially conservative. There was a clear pre-

20 Simon's early works normally contained the word 'portfolio' in the title to describe his estimates. However, his later works omit the phrase 'portfolio investment' in order to avoid confusion with the more exact definition of portfolio investment as a component of the long-term capital account of the balance of payments. I am indebted to Irving Stone for pointing this out.

TABLE 1.3
Canada's net capital inflow, estimates of Canadian new issues subscribed in Great Britain, and the stock of all British investment in Canada, 1890–1914

Year	Canada's net capital inflow (Hartland-Viner) ($ m)	Canadian new issues in Britain (Simon) ($ m)	Total British capital invested in Canada (Viner-Knox) ($ m)
(1)	(2)	(3)	(4)
1890	51.8	24.3	—
1891	54.4	26.2	—
1892	39.8	27.6	—
1893	40.8	23.3	—
1894	35.6	26.7	—
1895	31.3	9.2	—
1896	27.9	6.3	—
1897	10.5	18.9	—
1898	25.4	18.4	—
1899	36.4	10.2	—
1900	23.7	19.9	1,050.1
1901	41.7	9.2	1,065.2
1902	24.4	18.9	1,077.1
1903	48.5	10.2	1,105.9
1904	108.1	29.6	1,135.4
1905	94.0	71.3	1,211.8
1906	92.7	37.3	1,280.3
1907	156.9	32.0	1,345.5
1908	209.5	115.9	1,526.9
1909	173.4	116.9	1,739.6
1910	197.2	163.9	1,958.1
1911	332.7	143.6	2,202.5
1912	410.9	174.6	2,417.3
1913	412.7	238.6	2,793.1
1914	—	208.6	(2,778.5)*

SOURCES: The only presentation of the Hartland data in the form of a time series, which here is combined with the Viner data on net capital imports for the period 1900–13, is found in Bloomfield, App.1 42–3. This presentation of the Viner data on total British investment in Canada is taken from F.A. Knox, 'Excursus, Canadian capital movements and the Canadian balance of international payments, 1900–1934,' in H. Marshall *et al.*, *Canadian-American Industry* (New Haven, Conn., 1936), 299–300. The * marks the beginning of Knox's post-1913 series which is not perfectly contiguous with the Viner series. Simon, 'Canada,' 241

ference for government and government backed securities. Railroad bonds, where the bonds were guaranteed by the Canadian government, were a large component of this investment. The bonds of municipal governments in Canada were also significant, while only 5 per cent of the funds for manufacturing, fixed agricultural capital and livestock, and new building in Canada came from new issues floated in Great Britain. In terms of economic activity these sectors alone accounted for 63 per cent of all new Canadian investment. 'More adventurous British and especially American business groups used the method of direct investment to acquire, without security issues, a sizeable stake in Canadian industry and mining.'[21]

Although Hartland's evidence, in Table 1.2 suggests that by 1900 American direct investment in Canada was growing more rapidly than its British counterpart there is no reason to assume that it was more significant in every sector. As late as 1930 the stocks of direct investment of both Britain and the United States are roughly comparable in the financial sector.[22] This was after accelerating American investment for at least twelve years and a lack of British expansion.[23] Cleona Lewis, in an early Brooking's Institution study, estimated that British and American direct investment in Canada, net of that in manufacturing and railroads, was approximately equal.[24] Since American direct investment appeared to dominate all foreign investments in Canadian manufacturing there has tended to be, in the economic literature, a complete neglect of all British direct investment in Canada. It is the purpose of this study to show that this neglect has not been warranted.

METHOD

The estimates of British direct investment presented here are a critical adjunct to the description of British business enterprise in Canada. However, estimates are usually incomplete and not free from bias. In order that the reader may evaluate and possibly supplement the data of this study the collection and construction procedure is explained in some detail.*

21 Simon, 'Canada,' pp. 246-51
22 M.C. Urquhart and K.A.H. Buckley, *Historical statistics of Canada* (Toronto, 1965), p. 171
23 *Canada as a Field for British Branch Industries*, Department of Trade and Commerce (Ottawa, 1922), 1-24
24 Cleona Lewis, *America's stake in international investments*, The Brookings Institution (Washington, 1938), App. D., pp. 575-616. See Chapter III.
*A complete listing of the survey can be obtained from the author.

Definitions
Direct foreign investment is the additional resources provided to a host country through the actual transfer of funds, merchandise, or services from a foreign country through the agency of a foreign controlled firm.[25] The figures presented in this study are a measure of the financial or business capital raised by British firms and British controlled firms for direct investment purposes in Canada. Here, the term 'direct investment' refers only to equity securities and although a measure is given of the amount of bonds and other fixed-interest non-participating debt incurred by these firms it is not counted as direct investment. (The bonds floated by direct investments are an element in long-term portfolio foreign investment.) New direct investment is, then, the new issues of equities and the stock of direct investment is the value of the equities of all such firms under British control. The latter is a normally accepted financial method of measuring the amount of direct foreign investment. (No specific measurement is made of reinvested earnings to reflect the 'capital employed.')

As implied, the firm undertaking direct foreign investment had corporate status in at least the host country. Listed below are the four main types of legal structures for direct foreign investment.

Unincorporated branches An unincorporated branch is a company that operated in Canada with no separate legal status. These companies were required to register under the same corporate identity as in Great Britain where the head office was usually located.

Subsidiaries (a) A Canadian subsidiary company could be created and legal control retained by the holding of at least the required minimum of voting securities. (b) Subsidiary companies legally owned by other subsidiary companies in Canada are held to be under the same foreign ownership as the initial subsidiary. (c) A company registered solely in Canada may have been legally owned by foreigners who held a majority of shares privately. Although no corporate connection existed between Canada and Great Britain, this form is also held to be a direct foreign investment.

The corporate status of most British direct investments in Canada at this time was that of the unincorporated branch. For the purposes of analysis, however, it is necessary to distinguish between the various forms this company organisation took. First, a British company investing in Canada could be free from any corporate connections or

25 *The Canadian Balance of International Payments in the Post-War Years, 1946-1952*,, Dominion Bureau of Statistics (Ottawa, 1953), 85

informal connections, through the cross ownership of shares, with any other British company. Second, a company, such as Ridgway's (Canada) Limited carrying on a tea, coffee, and general provisions business, could be a British subsidiary company of a British parent company. In this case, almost four thousand of the five thousand registered shares were held by the parent, Ridgway's Limited.[26] Third, a company could set up a firm to undertake the parent company's activities in Canada with legal control vested in those individuals who also controlled the parent. This type of organisation was not uncommon in the family firm.[27]

It is also necessary to note that the unincorporated branch status of a firm indicates nothing about the extent of that firm's investment in Canada. A company's total activities could have been in Canada, with the exception of the registered office in Great Britain. Or a company may have been active in a country other than the host, usually the donor. Or, a company could have been totally or partially active in Canada during some phase of its existence. The existence of companies whose assets were only partly located in Canada presents problems in estimating direct investment. However, such firms were in a minority and are treated as exceptions, as will be noted later. The most important class of firms of this sort were those that acted in the host country simply as agencies to solicit sales for the companies' products which were normally manufactured in Great Britain. As will be seen later, up to 1914 the majority of direct investments of unincorporated branch status in this study invested solely in Canada for their entire lifetimes.

In Canada it is a convention, when calculating direct foreign investment, to exclude those Canadian companies which, although legally controlled by foreign investors, have a long historical record of being effectively controlled domestically. As distinct from legal control, effective control is exhibited by any holding of voting securities sufficient to control the company's financial structure. (If the majority of shareholders act independently of each other, irrespective of domicile, the minority interests which act together exhibit effective control.) Thus, although the majority of common shares and almost all of the preferred shares of the Canadian Pacific Railway were held in Great Britain, this investment should be properly counted as British

26 Ridgway's (Canada) Limited, *P.R.O.*, 96122/BT/31/18308
27 Wilkinson, Heywood, and Clark (British Columbia) Limited, *P.R.O.*, 119607/BT/31/20403

portfolio investment in Canadian equities since this company has always been effectively controlled by Canadian interests.[28] This policy has been adopted for all railroads.

Survey

The method adopted in this study to construct the estimates of British direct investment in Canada is to survey historical sources and build up information by isolating each firm that can be classified as a direct investment. This survey technique is, of course, analogous to the procedure used by most present-day central collecting agencies of governments. It has the distinct advantage of presenting measures of direct investment for the firm, any sector and, as far as the survey is complete, for the entire economy.

Foreign direct investment can currently be measured in Canada because of the existence of foreign subsidiaries. Since the most prevalent corporate form of investment in this time period was the unincorporated branch and since a specific check was made for holdings in subsidiary firms, direct investments can be equally well identified from either Canadian or British sources. Because of the varied requirements of company registration in Canada, falling under provincial jurisdiction, comprehensive lists of British direct investors from this source are impossible to obtain.[29] (In the case of some firms, registration was also required by the federal government. This was applicable to certain types of financial, transport, and shipping companies.) In some provinces the head office of the company was indexed with the name and registration number.[30] This then produced some evidence

28 *British and Foreign Direct Investments in Canada and Canadian Direct Investments Abroad, 1936*, Department of Trade and Commerce (Ottawa, 1938), 4

29 In most provinces all 'extra-provincial companies' were registered under the same section of the relevant companies legislation irrespective of whether the company was first registered in another province of Canada or another country. The chaotic nature of the records is typified by the division of the records of the then North-West Territories between Alberta and Saskatchewan in 1905. The New Brunswick government, which only required an annual report from British companies, also did not preserve these records until after 1938.

30 'Tabulated List of Companies Incorporated Licensed and Registered in the Province of British Columbia, made up to 31st October, 1913' in *Sessional Papers of British Columbia, 1919*, I (Victoria, B.C., 1913) B1–B104; *List of British Companies* (Quebec, 1969); *List of British Companies* (Manitoba, 1969); *List of British Companies* (Alberta, 1969). These *Lists* are in my possession.

of British direct investments in Canada. Similarly, the files of the Companies Registration Office of the Board of Trade in Great Britain do not lend themselves to the extraction of lists of overseas investments as all companies are indexed by name and registration number alone.

The initial list of direct investments was compiled from a systematic search of the main financial and specialized journals of the period. Among these was the *Stock Exchange Year-Book*, which gives a comprehensive coverage of all firms that ever issued, through stock exchanges in Great Britain, shares, bonds, or other securities. The other specialized journals listed in the bibliography were also used. The reporting coverage of these journals varied from extremely comprehensive notes in the *Mining Manual* to a list of a limited number of well-known Canadian investments in *Kitcat's Manual.* In addition to the investment journals, specialized newspapers such as the *Canadian Gazette* and the *Monetary Times*, which, from time to time, carried lists of British companies formed to invest in Canada, were used to supplement the lists of direct investments. Helpful also in this respect are the many newspapers cited in this study, which provided the same service for a sector of the economy such as mining. Trade directories too provided additional names of direct investments.[31]

From the initial information provided by these lists it was possible to identify those companies that either bought assets from or sold assets to British direct investments. These companies often turned out to be direct investments. At this stage the Canadian registration material could be used. Last, the records of the registered companies in Great Britain were surveyed by palpable title. This procedure did isolate other direct investments, but these were for the most part small or private companies. By this method a list of direct investments, or more properly, firms that were registered as intending to invest in Canada (only some of whom subsequently did so) was constructed. The completeness of the final list is open to question. However, the cross-checks with the Canadian registration data revealed that omissions were minimal and could be corrected. In this respect the British Columbia registration data are vital since it is only there that complete registration information for part of the period can be found. Similarly, the survey of the Quebec material covered many of the firms that were also registered in Ontario (where no information

31 For a list of the sources used, see the bibliography.

could be obtained) because of the requirement to register each company in every province where it carried out business activities.[32]

Assets

In order to identify a company as a direct investment, it is necessary to show that that company held assets in the host country, Canada. Assets were defined as any physical or non-physical asset that would require registration in the host country. They included capital, plant, machinery, inventories and property, as well as cash held in a bank located in Canada, options on property and mining claims, contracts of agents, and other non-physical assets. In the case of options on property it is likely that some British companies were not registered in Canada despite the requirement to do so.[33] Patents and licensing rights for Canada were not held to be assets unless the company was active in Canada since these patents did not require Canadian registration unless sold or used in Canada.[34]

Statements in a company's *Memorandum of Association* do not by themselves provide evidence of the existence of a company's assets, although such statements do provide valuable supporting evidence as well as peripheral information.[35] It was often necessary to trace a company's history beyond 1914 to provide the proof of assets in Canada. Finally, while the registration of a British company in Canada does not provide proof of actual assets held there, the appearance of a British company in the Canadian registration data provides a valuable guide to the fact that assets were held.

Sectors

The estimates and the analyses presented in this study are given at the sectoral level. Each firm was allocated to the sector that best described its main activity defined by its profit source. In practice, because specific information on profits for most firms was lacking, the principal asset determined the sector to which the company was

32 *List of British Companies*, B.C.; *List of British Companies*, Quebec; this last list was particularly useful in isolating British agencies active in Canada.

33 This would have been a clear violation of most companies' legislation in Canada, e.g. 'The Companies Act, 1910,' para. 168b of British Columbia.

34 In practice it is very difficult to distinguish between the rights to a process or distribution of a good or service unless it was actually employed in the host country, as often these rights were granted for North America and not specifically for Canada.

35 In the case of a public company it was a requirement that balance sheets be filed after 1907. Private companies did not have to submit a balance sheet to the Registrar of Companies in Great Britain.

assigned. For most firms this definition presented no difficulty since most British direct investments in Canada prior to 1914 were involved in only one activity. This designation of sectors closely follows the example of the business journals of the day and specifically that of the *Stock Exchange Year-Book*. Also, the definitions follow the needs to specify sectoral boundaries within which outputs are broadly similar and firms broadly comparable. Thus, the sectors as defined here are compatible with most contemporary studies.[36]

The single classification of a firm, despite the broad boundaries of each sector, gives rise to certain biases when that firm was involved in more than one activity in Canada. For instance, it may be argued that the Hudsons' Bay Company was a firm whose primary function was distributive. Historically this has been the case. However, during the time period under consideration, one of the main activities of this company was the sale of parts of its vast land holdings. In 1902 over half the company's net profit of $646,805 was derived from its land account. For the entire period to 1914 profits from the company's land account exceeded those from the fur and trading account, that is from its distributive function. Seventy-seven per cent of the company's largest yearly net profit in 1911 was attributed to the company's land sales.[37] Therefore, this company was classified as a land company and no account is taken of its distributive activities. This must, to some extent, be an arbitrary constraint. The same dilemma is faced when classifying firms into the subdivisions of each sector and the same rules are followed.

Eight sectors are used to define British direct investment in the Canadian economy of the period. These are: mining, oil and petroleum, land, timber, finance, distribution, utilities and service, primary and secondary manufacturing.

At various stages of this study it is necessary to examine a less aggregate grouping than the sector. Therefore, the mining sector is defined in terms of the main subdivision of gold, non-ferrous metals, non-metallic minerals, fuels, and miscellaneous types of mining activity. Similarly, urban land, rural land, miscellaneous real estate, mixed agriculture, and land selling activities, as well as pure agriculture define the subdivisions of the land sector. These subdivisions are simple divisions of the particular sector.

36 See for example, O.J. Firestone, *Canada's economic development, 1867–1953*, Incomes and Wealth, Series VII (London, 1958).

37 *Canadian industrial and miscellaneous companies* (London, 1912), p. 71

Specifically excluded from this study are some groups of companies normally considered to be direct investments. They are British registered charities, British shipping companies with agencies in Canada, and insurance companies. The two former categories were not usually required to be registered in Canada, and there is no evidence to suggest that they employed much capital in Canada. Insurance companies on the other hand formed a significant group of British investments. However, since the information on insurance companies is of a type inconsistent with the information used here and since this information has been presented in tentative estimates of the activities of insurance companies, they are not covered in this study. The contribution of British insurance companies has always been a moot point because of the lack of financial information and because of the problems connected with the valuation of assets and international investment portfolios in the host.[38] British investment in Canadian railroads is also excluded as a unique case and because of the convention of associating this investment with 'portfolio equities.'[39]

Measures

The main estimates presented in this study are all measures of aggregate business or financial capital. That is, they are measures of the amount of financial resources raised by the firm for the purposes of capital formation *and* current expenditure. With any aggregate financial information it is a hazardous procedure to identify a specific source of capital accumulation with specific uses of funds. This is so because of the existence of structural differences in firms through time, between firms in different sectors, between firms in the same sector, in firms of different sizes, and by the need of firms to generate 'working capital.'[40] However, direct foreign investment is a financial concept and only the financial aspects are discussed here.

38 Viner, pp. 110–12. For a commentary on the reports made by British insurance companies to the Canadian Federal government, see Urquhart and Buckley, pp. 252–63.

39 British investments, of all types, in Canadian railroads are included in the estimates of British portfolio investment in Canada in Simon, 'New British Investments in Canada, 1865–1914.'

40 D.H. Brill, 'Financing of capital formation,' *Problems of capital formation*, Studies in Income and Wealth, vol. 19, NBER (Princeton, N.J., 1957), pp. 147-9. It is also necessary to note the leakages, which would include such items as the cost of floating financial capital issues and the cost of maintaining a head office in Great Britain.

From the financial information gathered on each company three measures of the flow of British direct investment in Canada are compiled. These are (a) the nominal capital registered by the firms classified as British direct investments in any given year; (b) the paid-up capital measures the increases in the share issues credited as fully paid-up. This measure is adjusted to account for discounts and premiums; (c) the cash subscriptions calculated by deducting from (b) the value of shares issued for any purpose other than cash. In addition an estimate of the fixed interest debt issued by the firms is presented.

In order to account for the investment in British subsidiary firms in Canada, the share holdings of the parent firm are adjusted to the market price. Financial reconstructions also dictate an adjustment to reflect only the additional financial capital mobilized. With these modifications the nominal capital estimate measures the upper limit of firms to attract share capital and the upper limit of any financial investment. The paid-up capital estimate of new investment is that which best reflects the financial resources of direct investments, committed to projects in Canada, raised by the issue of share capital. It is on the basis of the paid-up capital that direct investment is usually measured because it represents the financial position of the company exclusive of incurred debt. It is this measure which is aggregated to reflect the stock of investment of firms active in a given year. The third estimate represents the funds committed by investors to this type of investment. Since issues for purposes other than cash may have had value, this is a lower biased estimate of the savings mobilized to invest directly in Canada.

The last type of estimate associated with British direct investment in Canada is the stream of dividends.[41] Cash dividends are readily identifiable as disbursements made in cash that do not affect the par value of the stocks issued at any stage of the company's life excepting those issued upon the liquidation of a company. Those 'dividends' issued upon the liquidation of a company properly represent a return *of* equity capital and not a return *on* equity capital and are not included in this definition of dividends.[42] Also specifically excluded were those dividends distributed by an amalgamated company after

41 See previous sources and *The Stock Exchange official intelligence*, London, various years, which provided a cross-check.

42 The best single source for information on equity capital returned after liquidation is found in *Register of defunct and other companies removed from the Stock Exchange Year-Book*, ed. W.S. Wareham (London, 1968).

a take-over since these dividends, issued as shares, represent a redistribution of assets with perhaps an increased par value, but do not represent cash payments. As presented, these cash dividends reflect closely the impact of repatriated profits on the balances of payments of both countries. Even although these dividends were issued, for the most part, in Great Britain, they represent an imputed measure of the outflow on Canada's current account under 'interest and dividends.'[43]

Possible Sources of Error

The evidence presented in this study is open to several sources of error. First, errors may be connected with the completeness of the survey. Second, errors of omission may occur because of the failure to identify assets held by any company in Canada. Steps were taken to minimize these potential errors.

The survey may lack completeness if certain types of reporting biases exist in the published sources used. These biases may be of three types: (i) a more accurate reporting of business activity over time, (ii) a cyclical bias in reporting at various stages of the business cycle, and (iii) more accurate reporting on certain sectors. Neither of the two major British journals, the *Mining Manual* and the *Stock Exchange Year-Book*, showed any strong bias for fuller reporting over time or any tendency to more or less accurate reporting at times of intense business activity. This was substantiated by cross-checks of both the Canadian and British registration data which were invariant to reporting biases. The completeness of the reporting in both these journals did vary and the *Stock Exchange Year-Book*'s reporting varied in some sectors. The *Mining Manual's* completeness may be judged by the absolute number of firms reported which failed to last long enough to carry out their declared intentions of investing in Canada and which, therefore, do not appear in the Canadian registration data. The cross-checks revealed an insignificant reporting error in the mining journal. Although restricted to reporting on firms that used the facilities of the British stock exchanges, the *Stock Exchange Year-Book* provided a wide range of coverage in all sectors except mining. There is a very complete coverage of most resource based and utilities overseas investments, as might be expected in view of

43 F.A. Knox, 'Excursus, Canadian capital movements and the Canadian balance of international payments, 1900–1934,' in H. Marshall, F.A. Southard, et al., *Canadian-American industry* (New Haven, Conn., 1936), pp. 308–11

historical British interests in these activities in areas such as Latin America.[44]

The smaller companies that did not use the stock exchange facilities were isolated by the procedures mentioned earlier and in turn cross-checked with the registration material. It is worth stressing that the variety of sources used, both British and Canadian, aid in eliminating the bias from any one source. The registration data provide a check and a final source. However, the registration material is, for the most part, composed of surveys, with the exceptions of the British Columbia and Manitoba records. Yet, because these latter records also contain companies that operated in other provinces of Canada, they provide a reasonably full report on all large companies as well as on small ones. For example, although Pilkington Brothers Limited operated mainly in Ontario, it is fully reported in the Quebec, Manitoba, and British Columbia registration data.[45] Therefore, it is likely that, if direct investments have not been isolated by the survey procedure, the companies concerned were small and that where such omissions occur they are randomly spread throughout the time period.

The second possible source of error is the failure to identify assets (previously defined) of companies known to have been direct investments in Canada. Despite the broad criteria used to define assets some cases could not be proven. For the most part, these firms were small public companies or private companies that did not invite subscriptions for shares or other securities. (This group seems to conform to the relative size of investment in each sector, except that no mining companies are included.)

There is also a group of British companies whose direct investments in Canada were part of wider investment activities in the United States. Normally, such companies can be isolated from the Canadian registration data. However, because the Canadian operations were of secondary importance, their balance sheets rarely report Canadian assets.[46] In order not to overestimate British direct investment in Canada, where no proof of Canadian assets exists, these companies have been excluded. (As noted earlier, where proof and infor-

44 J.F. Rippy, *British investments in Latin America, 1822-1949* (Hamden, Conn., 1966), p. 226

45 *List of British Companies*, Quebec; *List of British Companies*, Manitoba; *List of British Companies*, B.C.

46 For example, the Canadian and American Mortgage and Trust Company Limited, *P.R.O.*, 19341/BT/31/14759

mation on assets exist a value can be shown.) Typical of this type of problem was the Matador Land and Cattle Company Limited of Scotland which operated cattle ranches in the United States. Between 1905 and 1921 it owned a cattle ranch in Saskatchewan. No inference, however, can be made on the company's investment in Canada.[47] The extent of the underestimate in these two sectors cannot be measured. If the investments in Canada had been a large part of each company's investments, there would likely have been fuller disclosure in the balance sheets and more comment in the financial and specialized press.

The last element of the problem of identifying assets comes in distinguishing between direct investments which maintained agencies in Canada and those which operated manufacturing plants. Typically, this problem arises only in the instance of large British firms with small investments in the host country. This dilemma can be resolved by a cross-check with Canadian trade journals. The possibility remains that some firms classified here as agencies may have had small manufacturing plants in Canada. For example, a well-known British cigarette manufacturing company, isolated as a direct investment in Canada, simply listed in its balance sheet the item, 'Montreal Branch-Capital.' Since the item in question is small, $7,474, it has counted as an agency for the sale and distribution of the company's products rather than, say, a 'packaging plant.'[48]

Therefore, both possible sources of error act to render conservative the estimates of the number of British direct investments. It is unlikely that there is either a reporting or a cyclical bias in the time series presented. Furthermore, with the few exceptions noted above, slight under-estimates in the land and financial sectors and the possibility of switching between the distributive and manufacturing sector, the series, presented here are of the same degree of accuracy.

47 W.M. Pearce, *The Matador Land and Cattle Company* (Norman, Okla., 1964), pp. 150-1

48 Carreras and Marcianus Cigarette Company Limited, *P.R.O.*, 79802/BT/31/10559

2

New business enterprise

Throughout the nineteenth century Canadian capital imports originated mainly in Great Britain. These foreign savings financed much of the real capital formation, such as railroads in the 1850s, which became the foundation for increases in output and productivity.[1] Large capital inflows were dampened by the Grand Trunk fiasco[2] as British investors became reluctant to commit their savings to Canadian ventures. For most of the subsequent years to 1900 the average Canadian issue of securities in the British capital market remained below $20 million, with temporary up-swings in the early 1870s and late 1880s.[3] These years of reduced capital imports were the years of the national policy, a policy of internal development and high tariffs, which coincided with the so-called Great Depression.[4] Consequently, in the last quarter of the nineteenth century British investment was not sufficient to help Canada achieve a high rate of capital accumulation. This is indicated by the ratios of net domestic capital formation to net domestic product in 1870 and 1890 which were much lower than those of Australia or the United States.[5]

1 P. Hartland, 'Factors in economic growth in Canada,' *Journal of Economic History*, 15, no. 1 (1955), 14
2 W.T. Easterbrook and H.G.J. Aitken, *Canadian economic history* (Toronto, 1963), pp. 308–11
3 Simon, 'Canada,' pp. 241–3
4 Hartland, 'Factors,' 17
5 S. Kuznets, 'Long-term trends in capital formation proportions,' *Economic Development and Cultural Change*, 9, no. 4 (Part II, 1961), 1–24. John A. Stovel, *Canada in the world economy* (Cambridge, Mass., 1959), pp. 96-103. One of the better discussions of British capital exports is still, C.K. Hobson, *The export of capital* (London, 1914).

The well-known distribution of British investments in the Canadian infrastructure, especially in railroads, in the late nineteenth century, the conservative characteristics of this investment after the experience in the late 1850s, and its reduced absolute size resulted in an excess demand for capital in many sectors of the Canadian economy. Rapid expansion of transport and communication facilities through linkage effects induced a demand for capital in such sectors as manufacturing and agriculture. The mobilization of capital for these sectors remained a critical bottleneck in the Canadian economy throughout the nineteenth century.[6] Only to a limited extent did British portfolio capital exports satisfy this type of demand; during the years 1878–89 only 16.4 per cent of the British subscriptions to Canadian securities flowed into the non-public sectors.[7] In the private sectors – agriculture, land, finance, mining, and manufacturing – domestic saving were the main source of financial capital. Naturally, it was in the private sectors that foreign direct investment took place.[8]

Canada's slow but sustained rate of economic growth which had persisted from the 1870s began by the mid-1890s to exhibit more dynamic characteristics. In response to an increased world demand for primary products, Canadian exports of agricultural produce, minerals, and forest products more than doubled, in real terms, over the last ten years of the century, with the largest increases occurring after 1896. This was accompanied by a reversal in the terms of trade (export over import prices) in Canada's favour and by 1901 the wheat boom was evident. The growth of cereal agriculture and the expansion of farm acreage in western Canada provided much of the impetus for this new phase of economic development. Internal demand in the west helped to generate a growth in manufacturing in eastern Canada as well as stimulate a new phase of investment in the Canadian infrastructure. In turn, a boom in home building was experienced as the pace of urban development speeded up. Urban development was a consequence of the large net immigration into Canada at this time and the continuing rural-urban shift in both eastern and

6 C. Pentland, 'The role of capital in Canadian economic development before 1875,' *Canadian Journal of Economics and Political Science*, 16, no. 4 (1950), 461, cites the case in agriculture.

7 Simon, 'Canada,' p. 246

8 Lewis, pp. 293–5. Some American firms had been induced to jump the tariff of 1879 and fragmentary evidence suggests that most were manufacturing concerns. As will be seen later (Chapter 3), British direct investment was widely distributed across the private sectors.

western Canada. All these forces acted to produce a high and growing level of capital formation and a real annual rate of growth of total manufacturing output which averaged 6.0 per cent between 1900 and 1910.[9]

AGGREGATE NEW BRITISH DIRECT INVESTMENT

All of the measures of aggregate new British direct investment in Canada describe a similar pattern over the period 1890–1914 (Table 2.1). Two severe troughs occurred in 1894 and 1904 and two peaks in new investment in 1897 and 1912. The first peak was associated almost entirely with the mining boom in Canada whereas the second, at the height of pre-1914 prosperity, was composed of new investment activity widely distributed over various sectors. Of the financial capital paid-up in the years 1911 and 1912, 16.5 per cent was directed into mining, 18.4 per cent into land investment, 17.0 per cent into financial investment, 4.5 per cent into the utilities and service sector, and 41.0 per cent into manufacturing activities. Thus, the two peaks in new British direct investment in Canada between 1890 and 1914 were of very different types; throughout the period this new investment was becoming less concentrated in any one type of business activity.

New British direct investment in Canada was closely associated with the pattern of business activity within the Canadian economy (Table 2.2). Only during the mining boom of the late 1890s did this new investment peak at a different time from the Canadian business cycle. Later, when new British direct investment was less exclusive, there was a close correspondence with the pattern of general domestic economic activity. Throughout, the Canadian business cycle led (peaked and troughed before) the British reference cycle and the fact that new British direct investments more closely resembled the Canadian business cycle is evidence of the strong demand pull exerted.

If, however, the peaks and troughs of the nominal capital registered in Great Britain by *all* British companies are examined, a slightly different pattern emerges when compared with new British direct investment in Canada. This pattern suggests that within Great Britain favourable conditions in the capital markets for the registration of

9 Buckley (1955), p. 11. G. Bertram, 'Economic growth in Canadian industry, 1870–1915: the staple model and the take-off hypothesis,' *Canadian Journal of Economics and Political Science*, 29, no. 2 (1963), 170

TABLE 2.1
Estimates of aggregate new British direct investment in Canada, 1890–1914 ($000's)

Year	New companies registered	Nominal capital	Paid-up capital	Cash subscriptions	Bond issues
(1)	(2)	(3)	(4)	(5)	(6)
1890	8	12,449.9	2,965.8	2,495.8	517.4
1891	10	7,011.4	6,000.4	4,525.7	648.3
1892	6	3,140.4	2,075.9	1,033.2	389.9
1893	2	4,264.1	3,948.8	3,100.1	485.1
1894	3	515.7	776.0	533.5	77.6
1895	14	3,558.5	3,803.6	2,845.1	331.8
1896	39	20,711.7	12,114.2	4,930.5	931.5
1897	83	52,544.8	31,341.1	16,851.6	32.5
1898	70	39,103.6	30,712.8	15,118.6	639.2
1899	57	23,998.8	19,080.7	7,023.2	952.9
1900	38	25,906.0	23,216.5	16,638.2	185.8
1901	10	5,209.3	3,683.6	2,475.0	302.7
1902	15	7,517.7	6,572.7	2,014.2	1,544.8
1903	11	12,192.6	12,154.6	9,950.3	2,757.2
1904	6	773.3	505.4	130.5	539.9
1905	6	3,788.1	1,836.3	1,434.3	46.1
1906	25	16,129.5	11,198.4	7,867.5	956.1
1907	15	7,316.2	5,673.5	4,758.4	2,535.1
1908	19	19,404.7	14,438.0	3,540.5	6,161.9
1909	19	7,527.9	5,610.5	3,700.4	1,810.8
1910	42	34,159.2	19,126.1	15,283.1	10,991.9
1911	66	48,869.6	28,661.1	21,773.1	9,414.3
1912	50	54,961.5	48,143.1	23,555.4	12,047.4
1913	32	23,039.6	19,622.2	13,198.9	9,398.3
1914	22	24,819.2	14,742.0	13,005.4	634.9

For the sectoral estimates see Appendix A.

new equities had to exist before the demand for capital in Canada induced new British direct investment. This relationship is most obvious in the years from 1902 to 1906 when, despite the demand for capital in Canada, the unfavourable business conditions in Great Britain (measured by the willingness to register financial capital) precluded many new direct investments being formed (Table 2.3). New British direct investment in Canada, by any measure, was highly variable and new bond issues by British direct investments in Canada followed the same course. The only exception occurred in the period

TABLE 2.2
New British direct investment in Canada and Canadian and British business cycles, 1890–1914 (P/T = Peak/Trough)

Year	New British direct investment: paid-up capital	Canadian business cycle	British business cycle
(1)	(2)	(3)	(4)
1890	T	P	P
1891	P	T	—
1892	T	—	—
1893	P	P	—
1894	T*	T	—
1895	—	P	T
1896	—	T	—
1897	P*	—	—
1898	—	—	—
1899	T	—	—
1900	P	P	P
1901	—	T	T
1902	T	P	—
1903	P	—	P
1904	T*	T	T
1905	—	—	—
1906	P	P	—
1907	T	—	P
1908	P	T	T
1909	T	—	—
1910	—	P	—
1911	—	T	—
1912	P*	P	P
1913	—	—	—
1914	T	T	T

*Major turning points

SOURCES: A.F. Burns and W.C. Mitchell, *Measuring business cycles* (New York, 1946), 79–80; E.J. Chambers, 'Late nineteenth century business cycles in Canada,' *Canadian Journal of Economics and Political Science*, 30, no. 3 (1964), 391–412; K.A. Hay, 'Money and cycles in post-Confederation Canada,' *Journal of Political Economy*, June (1967), 266

1900–5 which can be attributed to the bond issues of mining companies after equity capital had become scarce. As might be expected, the bonds issued by the British direct investments show a more marked year to year variation than the bonds subscribed for all public

TABLE 2.3
Major turning points in the course of new British direct investment in Canada and all British company formation (P / T = Peak / Trough)

Year	New British direct investment in Canada turning points: nominal capital	Lead (+) or lag (-) of col. (2) with respect to turning points in the registration of nominal capital in Great Britain
(1)	(2)	(3)
1894	T	-1 years
1897	P	-1 years
1904	T	0
1912	P	-2 years

SOURCE: *Calculated from Statistical Abstract for the United Kingdom*, no. 51, 1889-1903 (London, 1904), 239 and no. 63, 1901-1915 (1916), 341

TABLE 2.4
British savings committed to British direct investments in Canada, selected periods 1890-1914

Period	$ 000's		
	Equities	Bonds	Cols. (3) ÷ (2) %
(1)	(2)	(3)	(4)
1890-1894	11,555.3	2,172.2	18.8
1895-1899	46,769.0	3,165.9	6.8
1900-1904	30,732.7	5,330.3	17.5
1905-1909	21,185.4	11,510.5	54.2
1910-1914	86,815.9	42,481.9	49.0

and private investment activity in Canada through the long-term portfolio capital account.

In summary, the periods 1895-9 and 1910-14 were those in which most British savings were mobilized for direct business participation in the Canadian economy. Also, throughout the years a growing amount of savings was used to purchase the bonds of the British direct investments in Canada. This reflected the growing diversity of business enterprise. Mining companies, unless they were large, seldomly floated bond issues and as the overall number of companies increased, especially after 1905, and as the relative number of mining companies fell, the bond-equity ratio became higher (Table 2.4). More financially complex companies were becoming involved in direct investment activity. These firms mobilized British savings in more than just the market for new equity issues.

DIVIDENDS

From 1890 to 1914 there were 117 British direct investments in Canada which issued dividends. The history of individual dividend issues varies widely from companies with continuous records of dividend payments to companies which only issued one dividend payment during their lifetime. As the number of British direct investments in Canada grew, the number of companies issuing dividends also grew, with peaks in 1901 and 1913. The aggregate dividend stream generated by these companies (Table 2.5), calculated as the cash dividends issued by British direct investments in all sectors, behaved in a cyclical fashion.

The pattern of the aggregate dividend stream generally conformed to the cyclical pattern of the stock of British direct investment (see Chapter 3). There were, however, some differences. Despite the increasing investment in the early years of the 1890s, the dividends declined steadily from 1890 to 1896 as first the existing companies lowered their individual payments and later the number of companies declined. Conversely, after the turn of the century, land and finance companies which had been active in the 1890s but had either not issued dividends, or kept these payments small, found themselves in a position to increase their dividend payments. Consequently, in the early years of the wheat boom the aggregate dividend stream varied less than the stock of investment. In the four years preceding the war the dividend payments of the newer companies did not achieve the same level as those issued by companies established prior to the 1910-14 boom. Thus aggregate dividends peak in 1911, four years prior to the largest stock of investment.

If each of the sectors is ranked by the proportion of total dividends from British direct investments (Table 2.6), the combined land and financial sectors dominate throughout the period except in the year 1900. Taken alone, the dividends from the financial sector were proportionately larger than those from the other sectors during most years of the 1890s. Mining dividends assumed pre-eminence only in 1899, 1900, and 1901 and from 1902 to 1912 the dividends from land investment ranked first. In the final two years of the period the

TABLE 2.5
Aggregate dividend payments from all British direct investments in Canada, 1890-1914

	Dividends ($'s)*	Returns of capital
(1)	(2)	(3)
1890	1,658,939	151,660
1891	1,566,671	—
1892	1,520,902	—
1893	1,555,644	—
1894	1,361,678	333,062
1895	1,334,348	—
1896	1,164,913	—
1897	1,262,194	—
1898	1,393,513	—
1899	1,963,829	—
1900	2,474,471	—
1901	2,003,600	—
1902	1,853,089	251,906
1903	2,303,761	1,187,814
1904	2,256,711	308,184
1905	2,540,960	146,198
1906	4,132,599	439,997
1907	4,645,646	—
1908	4,101,161	—
1909	4,789,551	—
1910	5,931,435	526,308
1911	7,544,850	—
1912	6,926,621	—
1913	7,005,545	—
1914	6,008,870	84,875

*Calculated on the basis of adjusting the dividends of the Mond Company Limited by the proportion of its assets in Canada

dividends from British direct investments in the manufacturing sector became predominant. This significant change in the stream of dividends from that sector which prior to 1913 varied between 0.6 and 12.9 per cent of the aggregate was due almost entirely to the dividend payments of one large company. In the last years of the 1900-10 decade the proportion of dividends from British direct investment in the Canadian utilities and service sector, which had been growing since 1899, overtook the proportion coming from mining and this position in the ranking was held until 1914. As a result, the composition of the dividend stream reflected the changing structure of investment.

TABLE 2.6
Dividends issued by British direct investments, by sectors, as a proportion of the total, 1890–1914*

	Sectors (%)							
	Mining	Oil	Land	Timber	Finance	Utilities & service	Mfg.	Total
	(1)	(2)	(3)	(4)	(5)	(6)	(7)	(8)
1890	6.4	—	31.9	—	53.5	—	8.1	100.0
1891	7.7	—	23.3	—	61.0	—	8.0	100.0
1892	6.0	—	24.5	—	64.5	—	5.0	100.0
1893	6.6	5.0	30.6	—	57.1	—	0.6	100.0
1894	11.7	5.8	26.9	—	51.6	—	4.1	100.0
1895	8.9	5.9	30.0	—	42.3	—	12.9	100.0
1896	10.6	—	33.2	—	46.7	—	9.5	100.0
1897	20.9	—	29.7	—	47.8	—	1.7	100.0
1898	29.7	0.8	29.3	—	31.7	—	8.5	100.0
1899	32.6	0.9	21.8	0.5	31.6	5.0	7.7	100.0
1900	48.8	0.7	19.4	—	20.0	4.0	7.2	100.0
1901	36.8	0.8	22.8	—	25.1	4.9	9.7	100.0
1902	16.4	0.8	40.2	—	27.1	5.8	9.6	100.0
1903	27.2	1.4	36.0	—	23.0	4.2	8.1	100.0
1904	12.2	0.8	47.9	—	23.9	8.1	7.1	100.0
1905	9.7	0.9	54.5	—	21.4	8.6	4.5	100.0
1906	13.7	0.5	56.0	—	15.1	7.7	7.1	100.0
1907	8.9	0.2	64.8	—	13.6	8.7	3.9	100.0
1908	13.3	0.2	51.8	—	15.5	14.6	4.7	100.0
1909	12.0	—	56.3	—	15.0	12.7	4.0	100.0
1910	9.0	—	61.5	—	14.1	11.6	4.0	100.0
1911	7.4	—	61.8	—	13.9	12.9	4.0	100.0
1912	11.8	—	44.9	—	18.5	14.4	10.3	100.0
1913	8.7	—	19.0	—	22.2	14.2	35.9	100.0
1914	17.8	—	24.6	—	17.0	10.7	30.1	100.0

*Dividends only

THE INTERNATIONAL SETTING

During the period 1890–1914 the secular growth in the amount of new British direct investment (paid-up capital) averaged $656.5 thousand per year. Departures from the secular trend conformed to a cyclical pattern over time which, as indicated earlier, produced sharp peaks and troughs. With only a few exceptions, new nominal capital varied more than new paid-up capital which, in turn, varied more than new cash payments from their respective trends. This variance confirms, in the aggregate, that those who were financing the new investment (through savings and, to some extent, through assets sold for shares) were less willing than the entrepreneurs to follow the booms. Thus, when new British direct investment in Canada is measured by the savings committed by the British public to finance these investments, it displays a dampened pattern of cyclical activity relative to the other measures of capital mobilization.

Normally new British direct investment moved in the same direction as new portfolio investment (British money calls on Canadian issues of securities). Apart from the irregularity of the mining boom in the years 1896 to 1900 which was ignored by the bond market, both British direct investment and portfolio investment appear to have been dominated by the same long swing in economic activity. The existence of this long swing is also confirmed by Hartland's data on Canadian net capital imports. That this cyclical activity was part of a wider international phenomenon is evidenced by the similar pattern traced out by British money calls on all foreign securities. Although British direct investment moved with British portfolio investment in Canada, it was more volatile, measured by percentage deviations from the secular trend. This was evident in the greater year to year fluctuations over the entire period 1890–1914. The causes of this greater variability lay in the exclusive business nature of this investment, which often tended to be concentrated within a narrow range of economic activities. Sectors such as mining and pastoral investment displayed by their performance sharper variations in growth than the rest of the economy. On the other hand, portfolio investment was spread across many institutional issues (governments), institutionally guaranteed issues, and business issues. Since these issues tended to be less risky than the equities issued by direct investments, they were less subject to fluctuations in the expectations of risk-takers. These fluctuations in expectations helped to generate sharp periods of boom and reaction to the boom. New British direct investment in Canada during the period 1890–1914 was the least stable form of long-term British investment in Canada.

The international economy of the years after 1870 was characterized by greater amplitudes in the nature of the long swings or Kuznets cycles than had previously existed in many areas of economic activity.[10] These long swings have already been observed in new British direct investment in Canada and the other data presented here. Most evidence suggests that the long swings in British net capital exports were induced by the pace of economic development in North America. Although these long swings were not simply confined to the North Atlantic area,[11] they were largely determined by the demand for capital in both the American and Canadian economies. (In many respects, economic development in Canada can be thought of as part of the wider development of North America.)[12] More and more after the 1880s it was the demand for British capital in Canada that helped to generate these cycles.

The mechanisms which appear to have transmitted these cycles were complex. Thomas has suggested that a substantial proportion of British capital formation was population sensitive (varying with the rate of population growth). Since labour, like capital, was in demand in the same phase of the cycle in the overseas country, it also contributed through emigration to the cyclical activity in British investment (or more properly gross domestic fixed capital formation).[13] In the United Kingdom down swings were, in part, offset by the expansion of exports. Productivity in the export sector increased because of the elasticity of supply of the factors shifting from the declining construction sector (a large contributor to gross domestic fixed capital formation). Eventually, as bottlenecks formed in the export sector, productivity declined and the terms of trade moved against Great Britain. 'On this reading of the interaction between the terms of trade and the inverse swing in home and foreign investment, one is

10 Williamson, 200

11 Bloomfield, pp. 8–9, H. Abramovitz, 'The nature and significance of Kuznets cycles,' *Economic Development and Cultural Change*, 9, no. 3 (1961), 225–8; K. Martin, 'Capital movements, the terms of trade and the balance of payments,' *Bulletin of the Oxford University Institute of Statistics*, 11, no. 11 (1949), 357-66

12 J.H. Young, 'Comparative economic development: Canada and the United States,' *American Economic Review*, 45, no. 1 (1955), 80–93

13 B. Thomas, 'The historical record of international capital movements to 1913,' in *Capital movements and economic development*, ed. J.H. Adler (London, 1967), p. 21

led to regard movements in the net barter terms of trade as a consequence of the fundamental forces at work rather than a causal factor determining the distribution of the flow of capital between home and foreign investment.'[14] The fundamental forces were the push-pull on British capital and labour from the United States and Canada (along with some other countries).[15]

Given these long swings, it would be expected that new British direct investment would be positively related to the returns from past investment, dividends, and negatively related to British home investment. Equation (1) confirms that these fundamental pull and push forces explain a significant proportion of the variations in new direct investment.

$$DI = 2797.513 + 2.829\mathrm{D}_t - 421.969 I^{\mathrm{GB}}_{t-4} - 84.216T \qquad (1)$$

$$(1.643) \quad (-2.350) \quad (-0.689)$$

$$\text{D.W.} = 1.445 \quad R^2 = 0.540,$$

where DI = the new cash subscription to British direct investments,
D = the aggregate dividend stream,
I^{GB} = gross domestic capital formation in Great Britain,
and T = time and the parenthesis enclose t - statistics.

Because new investment did not generate dividend payments for at least one year, no dual causality exists in the above relationship. British direct investment on balance was slow to respond to Canadian investment opportunities. D is implicitly a lagged proxy for Canadian domestic investment.

Since D represents an index of economic activity in Canada, it would be supposed that such movements in conjunction with British home investment would also explain the measured capital inflow and new British portfolio investment.

$$K = 11.379 + 0.255\mathrm{D}_t - 10.630 I^{\mathrm{GB}}_{t-1} - 2.685T \qquad (2)$$

$$(2.267) \quad (-0.816) \quad (-0.423)$$

$$\text{D.W.} = 1.806 \quad R^2 = 0.697,$$

where K = Hartland's estimate of Canadian gross capital imports.

14 Thomas, p. 29
15 Bloomfield, p. 23

$$S = 27.897 + 0.011D_t - 3.129I_t^{GB} + 0.905T \qquad (3)$$

$$(1.106) \quad (-2.647) \quad (1.815)$$

$$\text{D.W.} = 1.137 \quad R^2 = 0.829,$$

where S = Simon's estimate of all new Canadian securities issued in Great Britain.[16]

$$Sp = 11.663 + 0.011D_t - 1.756I_{t-4}^{GB} + 0.438T \qquad (4)$$

$$(2.011) \quad (-3.243) \quad (1.189)$$

$$\text{D.W.} = 2.067 \quad R^2 = 0.864,$$

where Sp = Simon's estimate of new Canadian securities issued by private businesses in Great Britain.

On the basis of the above evidence it can be argued that the exogenous forces (such as the closing of the American frontier and the increasing wheat prices of the 1890s) which caused the expansion in Canada stimulated the demand for capital. The response to the pace of Canadian development came in the form of capital flows which amplified cyclical activity in both countries. It was the divergence in business opportunities that then stimulated a flow of new direct investment funds. Throughout the long swing in the period 1890–1914, new British direct investment in Canada was, like Canadian net capital imports, determined both by the British search for alternative investment opportunities overseas and by the pull of the demand for capital in Canada. The slower response of new British direct investment to the long swing in British gross domestic fixed capital formation was in part the slowness of businessmen to recognize business opportunities in Canada, a reflection of the variety of individual businesses involved, and the less perfect capital market in which the funds were raised. Earlier it was noted that new British direct investment in Canada was dominated by the country's business conditions and did

16 The U.S. result presented by Williamson for the period 1890–1914 is

$$K_t = 699.2 + 0.404I_t^{US} - 616934I_t^{GB}, \; R^2 = 0.891$$

where K_t is United States net capital imports and I is investment. These results have been confirmed by von Tunzleman in this simple form. The transformations he suggests were carried out unsuccessfully on the equations presented here; Williamson, 148, and G.N. von Tunzleman, 'The new economic history: an econometric appraisal,' reprinted in *The new economic history*, ed., R.L. Andreano (New York, 1970), pp. 162–8

not appear to be regulated by the British business cycle. This is consistent with the influence of home investment in Great Britain as a determinant of the long run behaviour of the time pattern of new British investment in Canada. All British capital exports from 1870 to 1914 tended to move inversely with British home investment over the short run as well as over the long run.[17] This was also true of that investment, portfolio and direct, in Canada over the period 1890–1914. However, the tendency for new British investment in Canada to increase at the expense of home investment in the short run in Great Britain was a consequence of, rather than a determining factor limiting, the pull of the demand for capital in Canada.

In the case of new British direct investment a highly complex relationship governed the mobilization of financial capital. As seen previously, certain business conditions (not necessarily the phase of the business cycle) in Great Britain, such as a buoyant share-price index and market for equity capital, facilitated this new investment. For instance, during the mining boom of 1896–1900, investment was contingent upon a rising share-price index and a mood of optimism in the registration of all new nominal share capital. During the early years of the 1900s, it was the depressed nature of those business conditions which helped to constrain the amount of new British direct investment in Canada. The rising amount of new investment in Canada after about 1906 was stimulated further by the general improvement in share prices after 1909. Such favourable business conditions were not necessary either for the total new placement of foreign security issues or the new placement of Canadian security issues in Great Britain.

In summary, although for the period 1890–1914 as a whole new British direct investment in Canada was simply the sum of the individual actions of British entrepreneurs, it did display distinct aggregate characteristics. Over the entire period this new investment displayed the evidence of a long swing from a peak in about 1890 to another peak in the immediate pre-1914 period. This new investment was the main impetus for the cyclical quality of the stock of British direct investment in Canada.

17 Bloomfield, p. 22. Bloomfield's evidence confirms the negative relationship between the first differences of British net capital exports and British investment; Simon, 'Canada,' pp. 252–4.

PROMOTIONS AND PUBLICITY

Although the British capital market defies any precise delineation and each entrepreneur promoted his Canadian investment project in his own way, it is still possible to distinguish two different methods used to mobilize financial capital. First there were those firms that employed the services of the financial institutions, such as the stock-exchanges, and second those that relied on the 'traditional' methods of selling equity securities. The latter activity was chiefly characterized by (i) appeals to family and business colleagues for subscriptions, (ii) promotional activities in a specific geographic area away from the main financial centres, and (iii) flows of information by personal rather than institutional means. There are two dimensions to the information problem. How was it channelled from Canada to Great Britain and how was it spread in the capital market?

One of the principal mechanisms by which the influence of certain companies was brought to bear on the course of new British direct investment in Canada was through the activities of the stock exchanges. This was accomplished in two main ways. First, the market value of the equity and fixed-interest securities was set primarily by their trading on the British stock exchanges. Although very few companies were quoted regularly, general trading established market prices, based on the companies' performances, which directly indicated to potential new investors the general appraisal of each company's profitability. Second, because a company used a stock exchange's facilities there was usually information available, in publications such as the *Stock Exchange Year-Book*, and the general financial press, about its business activities, assets, and dividends. Entrepreneurs and potential investors could assess this information to decide whether one company's experience, or the collective experience of many companies, was a suitable demonstration of their prospects. They would then act accordingly.

As can be seen from Table 2.7 the shares of relatively few British direct investments in Canada were regularly quoted on the stock exchanges. In 1914 only 33 of the 203 active, non-mining companies were listed consistently. (In addition, only nine mining companies had their shares quotes regularly on the London stock exchange.) Many more companies, however, used the facilities of the stock exchange both to issue new equities and bonds and to establish a market where the holders of those securities could trade. In the financial

TABLE 2.7
Number of British direct investments which at any time used the facilities of the British stock exchanges, selected years (excluding mining companies)

Years	Oil	Land	Timber	Finance	Distrib.	Utilities & services	Mfg.	Total
(1)	(2)	(3)	(4)	(5)	(6)	(7)	(8)	(9)
	Number in sector							
1890	1	23	1	11	—	2	4	42
1895	3	20	1	13	—	2	7	46
1900	5	22	4	14	4	9	16	74
1905	5	24	4	11	4	12	14	74
1910	10	41	5	23	6	10	18	113
1914	13	99	7	40	7	16	21	203
	Number using exchanges							
1890	1	15	2	11	2	1	4	36
1895	2	16	1	13	—	1	8	41
1900	3	15	2	15	—	6	11	52
1905	4	16	2	11	—	9	10	52
1910	6	23	4	18	—	9	10	70
1914	7	38	4	29	1	6	9	94
	Number with share prices quoted							
1890	—	8	—	6	—	—	1	15
1895	—	7	—	6	—	—	2	15
1900	—	6	—	6	—	1	2	15
1905	—	7	—	5	—	1	2	15
1910	—	12	—	10	—	1	4	27
1914	—	15	—	13	—	1	4	33

SOURCE: *The Stock Exchange Year-Book*, various issues

sector most companies that invested in Canada throughout the period 1890–1914 used the facilities of the stock exchanges. This was a reflection of the fact that the financial companies were on average much larger than any of the other British direct investments in Canada at this time. They were larger in terms of both the average paid-up capital and the amount of bonds and other debt instruments they employed. Therefore, they had a much greater need for appeals to the general public than many other companies.

In part the successful flotation of certain of the British companies using the facilities of the stock exchanges was due to the existence of the large speculative element associated with Canadian mining and land ventures. This speculation in the shares of existing British direct investments was primarily based on the possibility of the appreciation of their market value. Although few of the shares were quoted regularly, there was a highly organized market in the London stock exchange for some of these speculative issues. The usual trading place for the shares in the mining firms investing in the Canadian mining booms was, reputedly, next to the 'Kaffir market' (the market trading in South African mining shares).[18]

The speculation on the capital appreciation of shares itself did not lead to an increase in the amount of capital paid-up for any individual British direct investment in land or mining. However, a general mood of optimism (speculation in an appreciating market) led to a condition that favoured the increased participation of new companies. (The correlation coefficient between the overall British share index and the number of newly registered companies at the Board of Trade was 0.707 for the 1890–1914 period.) When this optimism was related directly to risk-taking economic behaviour, speculation resulted. Occasionally this speculation was rewarded by an increased capital value and occasionally it was supplemented by a large lump-sum payment, from an Anglo-Canadian mining company, which in turn helped to sustain the speculative boom. The Yukon Goldfields Limited issued a dividend of twenty per cent shortly after registering the company (which acquired an existing mine) and called for a premium on the 6,185 shares about to be issued.[19] The market price was forced up.

18 E.V. Morgan and W.A. Thomas, *The Stock Exchange; its history and functions* (London, 1962), p. 97

19 *Yukon Goldfields* (A Report to the Shareholders of the Yukon Goldfields Ltd.), dated 19 December 1899, *British Museum*

The period of most active trading and speculation in the shares of Anglo-Canadian mining companies was during the British Columbia-Yukon mining boom of 1896 to 1900. For the shares in British land companies in Canada the most active period was during the years 1909 to 1913 at the height of the wheat boom. These were also the most active periods for the subscription of new paid-up capital to such firms. In each case, by 1899 and 1913 respectively there was a reaction to the boom.[20] In part this was the inevitable consequence of profits not keeping pace with high and rising expectations. However, the decline in the new capital subscriptions was hastened in each of the periods of reaction to the booms by the revelation of the activities of a major British company.

In 1899 the collapse of a British company, the London and Globe Finance Corporation Limited, a holding company for several British direct investments in Canadian mining, brought to light some dubious practices on the part of the mining companies. 'The fact stands out clearly that both the London and Globe and the British American Corporation were making transactions on paper only (i.e. on the transfer of Canadian mining assets), and were together with the Standard Exploration Company using their cash and assets in gambling shares in the Stock Exchange.'[21] The London and Globe Finance Corporation and the British America Corporation were voluntarily wound up, subject to the supervision of the Court. The mining market appears to have been shocked by the disclosures.[22] Yet the Canadian mining assets of the firms involved in the debacle were basically sound. The Le Roi No. 2 Limited, originally formed by the British America Corporation, after changing its managerial policy, had become a respected mining company by mid-1903[23] and, by 1910, was one of the largest Anglo-Canadian companies in British Columbia, producing about 30,000 tons of gold-silver-copper ore per year.

Similarly, the liquidation of the Canadian Agency Limited in 1913 helped to shake the remaining confidence in the last stages of the land boom. This company was forced into liquidation by the collapse

20 For mining companies very little evidence records the share prices. There is, however, more evidence on the share prices of Anglo-Canadian land companies which suggests that the shares of the large companies declined less than some of the others. However, in both booms, as noted earlier, new subscriptions of capital were quickly curtailed after 1900 and 1913 respectively.

21 *The Canadian Mining and Mechanical Review*, 30 November (1901), 236

22 *The Statist*, 8 June (1901), 1062

23 *The Statist*, 2 May (1903), 936

of one of its subsidiary companies (British not Canadian). The subsidiary had operated in Alberta and collapsed when it could not meet the interest expenditures. The liquidation revealed a deficiency of \$53.5 million in the assets of the parent company. Up to June 1913 it had reported profits of over \$2.5 million and distributed dividends of over \$2 million. But, 'the receiver observes that the amount of profits shown for the last four years is questionable, inasmuch as the securities, which were revalued each year for the purposes of the balance sheet were of a speculative nature.'[24] The company left debts of over \$5 million.

Both these revelations immediately dampened speculative activity on the capital appreciation of shares. Many potential entrepreneurs became reluctant to register new companies and those who did found the British public less willing to subscribe their savings. In this manner both the London and Globe Finance Corporation Limited and the Canadian Agency Limited helped to bring a speedy end to the booms in British direct investment in the Canadian mining and land sectors.

There were a great many British companies which undertook direct investment in Canada without resorting to the organized capital market of the stock exchanges. In the mining and land sectors, syndicates owned by small groups of businessmen were popular. All three of the shareholders of the Toronto and Montreal Syndicate Limited were listed as 'financiers' of London.[25] Many other companies refrained from inviting the public to subscribe to share issues but had more shareholders than the syndicates. Typically the entrepreneurs of such firms mobilised the savings of business associates, friends, and family. The Scottish Canadian Trust Limited of Dundee, formed in 1907, had only four major shareholders. Two were owners of a jute mill (both named Sharp) and the others a shipowner and a newspaper proprietor (both named Thompson).[26]

Prospectuses were often issued by companies but circulated to specific individuals. Virtually all of the shares (£50,000) of the Carlisle Canning Company Limited were held by local businessmen in the north of England. The Bolton subscribers included cotton mill owners, tea merchants, brewers, corn millers, and various other manufacturers.[27] Often the prospectus was widely circulated within a given

24 *The Monetary Times*, 19 February (1915), 20
25 Toronto and Montreal Syndicate Limited, *P.R.O.*, 128694/BT/31/21424
26 The Scottish Canadian Trust Limited, *S.C.R.O.*, 6394
27 The Carlisle Canning Company Limited *P.R.O.*, 7259/BT/31/51342

geographic area. Much reliance was placed on the informal passing of information from one individual to another. So publicized, the majority of the equity in the Bristol and West of England Canadian Land Mortgage Company Limited was taken up by residents of Bristol and nearby Clifton. This company also typified the informal communication processes often evident between individuals in Canada and Great Britain. The Bristol and West of England company was first promoted by a group of Toronto real estate brokers, but a prosperous Bristol merchant, later secretary of the company, mobilized the financial capital.[28] In British Columbia it was a local entrepreneur, R.B. Venner, who initiated the land investment company promoted by a member of his family in London.[29] In a small silver mining company the only Canadian shareholder (and manager) had the same name as two members of the board of directors.[30] The evidence supports the view that some of the British direct investments, especially the smaller ones, were initiated by Britons who had migrated to Canada in the late nineteenth century. Only occasionally did Canadian promoters with no strong British connections solicit financial capital. J.J. Banfield of British Columbia, an insurance and financial agent, promoted several companies in the Liverpool area for investment in real estate and mortgages by journeying to England and personally drumming up support.[31]

Brought into being by British capitalists acting on information conveyed through informal and irregular channels, it can be imagined that many new firms were created with insufficient evidence of probable success. Many small firms were formed in haste, a fact often reflected in their financial structures. Others were created in response to a demand long since changed, as was the case of a small building company which became active in British Columbia long after the 1913 building boom has collapsed.[32] Yet, despite the variety of mechanisms, formal and informal, used to mobilize financial capital, the aggregate for direct investment purposes in Canada was such that it exhibited an identifiable regularity.

28 The Bristol and West of England Canadian Land Mortgage Company Limited, *P.R.O.*, 2415/BT/31/12141

29 The Victoria (B.C.) Land Investment Trust Limited, *P.R.O.*, 20811/BT/31/123270

30 The Murillo Silver Mine Limited, *P.R.O.*, 4578/BT/31/29976

31 H.J. Boam, *British Columbia, its history, people, commerce, industries and resources* (London, 1912), p. 208

32 British and Canadian Builders Limited, *P.R.O.*, 133259/BT/31/21970, letter to the Registrar of Companies from the company secretary, 15 Sept. 1927

3

The stock of British direct investment in Canada

Contemporary observers had long been aware of the business activities of foreigners in Canada but it was not until after the World War I that the full extent of this investment was realized. The post-war evidence revealed that British direct participation in the Canadian economy had not grown at the same rate as American in the early twentieth century and to many, including the officials of the Department of Trade and Commerce, this evidence could not be adequately explained.[1] In this chapter new estimates of the stock of British direct investment in Canada are presented which make possible an assessment the extent and vitality of British business enterprise.

PRE-1890 INVESTMENT

At the end of 1889 there were 64 active British direct investments in Canada with an aggregate paid-up capital of $42.0 million (Table 3.1). For the most part, this investment was concentrated in mining, real estate, and financial concerns. Other sectors of the Canadian economy had received scant attention from British entrepreneurs, especially manufacturing which by this time registered at least 32 American branch plants mainly in the textile and metal working industries.[2] Since much of British business activity in the 1880s had been directed

1 This pattern of direct foreign investment [1922] contained within it 'a certain regret for Canadians, perhaps only now commencing to be felt; it is that manufacturers of the United Kingdom are taking so little part in the industrial development of the country ... and the hope of Canadians is that the Dominion may develop in the future as it has in the past, along British lines.' *Canada as a field for British branch industries*, intro.

2 Lewis, pp. 293–5

TABLE 3.1
Stock of British direct investment in Canada at the end of 1889, by sector and province ($000's)

Sector	Companies: Number	Companies: %	Nominal capital	%	Paid-up capital	%
(1)	(2)	(3)	(4)	(5)	(6)	(7)
Mining	23	35.9	9,711.1	14.0	6,896.5	16.4
Oil and Petroleum	1	1.6	1,938.5	2.1	1,938.6	4.6
Land	23	35.9	24,182.7	34.8	17,930.2	42.7
Timber	2	3.2	604.8	0.9	538.8	1.3
Finance	8	12.7	26,382.8	38.0	11,503.5	27.4
Distribution	2	3.2	3,152.5	4.5	1,255.7	3.0
Utilities	2	3.2	1,018.5	1.5	750.1	1.8
Manufacturing	3	4.8	2,473.5	3.6	1,153.7	2.7
TOTAL	64	100.0	69,463.9	100.0	41,966.8	100.0
Provinces						
British Columbia	17	27.0	8,292.9	11.9	6,939.6	16.5
Alberta	5	7.9	3,454.2	5.0	725.3	1.7
Saskatchewan	3	4.8	1,503.5	2.2	634.8	1.5
Manitoba	8	12.7	8,588.3	12.4	2,303.8	5.5
Ontario	9	14.3	6,155.0	8.9	3,101.5	7.4
Quebec	7	9.5	5,701.8	8.2	2,262.9	5.4
Nova Scotia	4	6.3	3,441.2	5.0	3,259.0	7.8
N.B. and P.E.I.	1	1.6	1,455.0	2.1	766.3	1.8
Canada, unassigned	10	15.9	30,872.6	44.4	21,974.2	52.4
TOTAL	64	100.0	69,463.9	100.0	41,966.8	100.0

TABLE 3.2
Eight oldest British direct investments in Canada operating in 1889

Name	Date	Paid-up capital $000's	Type of organization
(1)	(2)	(3)	(4)
1 Hudson's Bay Company	1670	6,305	Royal Charter
2 General Mining Assoc. Ltd.	1825	1,067	Limited Liab. 1868
3 Canada Company	1826	40	Royal Charter
4 British American Land Co.	1834	733	Royal Charter
5 Bank of British North America	1836	4,850	Royal Charter
6 Trust & Loan Company of Canada	1845	1,576	Royal Charter
7 Bank of British Columbia	1862	2,910	Royal Charter
8 Vancouver Island Coal Mining and Land Company Ltd.	1862	897	Limited Liab.

to land and financial investments, it tended to be diffused throughout the country, mainly in the central and western regions, with British Columbia being the favoured location for single enterprise firms.

Two distinct types of British companies operated in Canada in 1889. First, there were the older, established companies such as the Hudson's Bay Company and the Canada Company which traced their origins to monopolies and exclusive franchises granted under the Colonial régime. Six companies of the eight founded prior to Confederation continued to function with royal charters throughout the pre-1890 period (Table 3.2). However, most of the British direct investments were of more recent origin and had been formed under the limited liability provisions of British company law which had been revolutionized in the early 1860s.[3] These firms were essentially modern in character and exhibited a variety of financial structures from the single-owner firm to the complex, publicly subscribed company. Despite the emergence of the new corporate forms, most British business enterprises in Canada continued to function without separate Canadian incorporations; their legal status was that of the unincorporated branch. All such firms maintained head offices in Great Britain. This practice, so strongly evident in the mid-nineteenth century, was to remain the dominant legal characteristic of British business enterprise in Canada until at least 1914.

3 Schmitthoff, pp. 5-10

Of the 23 British mining companies active in Canada at the end of 1889 most were of recent origin. Only in coal mining were the businesses of older establishment. For example, the General Mining Association Limited was founded in 1825 and first registered with limited liability in 1868. Formed to work leasehold property in Sydney, Nova Scotia, this company operated for seventy-five years, produced regular dividends and on four occasions reduced the par value of its shares by granting cash refunds. In the west the successful [New] Vancouver Coal Mining and Land Company Limited pre-dated Confederation. When liquidated in 1902 the Nanaimo mines and 30,000 acres of property on Vancouver Island were sold for over half a million dollars in cash. Apart from such notable exceptions few of the pre-1890 British mining ventures were either profitable or long-lived; the average age at liquidation was under seven years. Nevertheless, there were exceptions and two British direct investments in metallic mining formed in the eighties survived into the twentieth century.

Although equal numbers of companies were active in both the mining and land sectors, real estate and related agricultural business accounted for a much larger proportion of the stock of British direct investment in Canada by 1889. Part of the investment, however, was in the well-known but generally unsuccessful colonization companies of the 1880s.[4] Of these the largest surviving at the beginning of 1890 were: Canada Homestead Settlement Company Limited; Canada and North-West Land Company Limited; Canadian Agricultural, Coal and Colonization Company Limited; Canadian Co-operative Colonization Company Limited; and Canadian Pacific Colonization Corporation Limited. All but the first were liquidated by 1896. Other large companies of this type, like the Scottish-Canadian Land and Settlement Association, had collapsed in the late 1880s.[5] These particular British firms were based on the attraction of specific groups of settlers and the sale of land in organized community structures. The Canadian Agricultural, Coal and Colonization Company Limited specialized in trying to attract 'high class' farm labour and the younger sons of English farmers with at least $2,500 capital. This company met total expenditures in Canada of over $717 thousand before going into liquidation. The failure of the early British colonization land companies generally stemmed from their inability to overcome the physical con-

4 N. Macdonald, *Canada, immigration and colonization 1841–1903* (Aberdeen, 1966), p. 247

5 Macdonald, p. 245

ditions of prairie farming. They also failed to attract immigrants in face of the tide of immigration into the USA. In the anticipation of certain levels of land sales, expenditures were undertaken which could not be met when the uncertain demand produced land prices below those expected. Other colonization companies dedicated to cattle ranching activities, rather than to growing cereals or mixed farming, lost their land leases when they too failed to attract enough settlers.[6]

In the western settlement of Canada cattle ranching in the fertile areas generally preceded mixed and cereal farming. This segment of agriculture was subject to certain contradictory pressures. Since land was in great demand for cereal agriculture the ranchers were dispossessed in many areas. Facilitating the dispossession was the practice of the Crown and other major land holders of granting grazing rights for only short periods of time, normally two years. In Britain the demand for Canadian beef had been growing since the late 1870s. However, the British government at various times in the 1880s, and later in the 1890s, threatened embargos against the importation of live Canadian cattle. Thus, the British importers, who usually fattened the cattle after their arrival in Britain were constantly in fear of administrative fiat.[7] The uncertainty caused by the short leases and import restriction possibilities in Britain meant that British direct investments in cattle ranching in Canada never became as significant as those in the USA where there was a substantial internal market. By the end of 1889 only two major investments of this type undertook production in Canada.[8] These two companies had managed to avoid the land pressure. The Sweet Water Ranche and Supply Company of Leeds, England Limited survived until 1891 when it sold its land leases and its stock intact to another ranching company.[9] On the other hand, the New Oxley (Canada) Ranche Company Limited with-

6 Canadian Pacific Colonization Corporation Limited, *P.R.O.*, 25997/BT/31/4485

7 'Evidence on the Export Cattle Trade of Canada,' Department of Marine and Fisheries, Sessional Papers, No. 78 (Ottawa, 1891), 7-8. This uncertainty caused many companies that were formed to carry out both the production of cattle in Canada and their importation into Britain to liquidate in desperation. Canadian Cattle Company of Aberdeen Limited, *S.C.R.O.*, 1753 Diss.

8 For this investment in the U.S.A., see W. Turrentine Jackson, *The enterprising Scot, investors in the American West after 1873*, Edinburgh, 1968 and W.M. Pearce, *The Matador Land and Cattle Company*, Norman, Oklahoma, 1964.

9 Sweet Water Ranche and Supply Company of Leeds, England Limited, *P.R.O.*, 25269/BT/31/3978

stood the uncertainty but significantly did not issue a dividend until 1898, twelve years after its registration.

The most successful group of British direct investments in land, in terms of avoiding voluntary or compulsory liquidation, were those companies in the province of Manitoba. In all, six companies operated there exclusively or directed their other interests from that province. This survival appears to be directly related to the intensive (as compared to Alberta and Saskatchewan) land settlement in Manitoba, one of the first areas of the prairies to be open for settlement, compared to Alberta and Saskatchewan. The only company that operated exclusively in Ontario was the Canada Company which still maintained some land holdings in the well-populated regions of Southern Ontario. Although this company had reduced its nominal capital to only $40,347 by 1889, its shares in 1890 and throughout the 1890-1914 period were traded on the London market at substantial premiums.[10]

Finance was the second largest sector of British direct investment at the beginning of 1890, accounting for 27.4 per cent of the stock. This was concentrated in eight companies, two of which were banks, one a trust and loan company, and the other five associated with the mortgage loan business.

Both the British banks in Canada had been formed before 1867. The Bank of British Columbia had been active in the far west and participated in the earlier gold rushes in British Columbia. In 1890, the bank operated six branches in western Canada and maintained a level of total bank deposits of over $2.3 million. The Bank of British North America operated more extensively throughout Canada and ranked as the country's second largest bank, on the basis of the level of paid-up capital, in the period immediately after Confederation. Although it did not grow at the same pace as the domestic banks, it was still one of the larger banks in 1890, maintaining a level of total bank deposits of $8.3 million.[11] Together these banks accounted for approximately 8.4 per cent of all deposits in the Canadian banking sector.[12] Despite the leading position of one of these banks, no other attempts were made during the 1867-90 period to establish new British direct investments in banking. Even the attempts by Canadians, prior to 1890, to form colonial banks based partially in London

10 *The Stock Exchange Year-Book*, various issues

11 R.M. Breckenridge, *The Canadian banking system, 1817-1890* (New York, 1895), pp. 119-20, 464-9

12 Total deposits from Urquhart and Buckley, p. 241

TABLE 3.3
Stock of British direct investment in Canada, 1890-1914 ($000's)

Year	Number of active businesses	Nominal capital	Paid-up capital
(1)	(2)	(3)	(4)
1890	64	75,548.1	42,981.1
1891	70	81,385.9	46,844.8
1892	74	84,353.6	48,832.4
1893	70	74,598.4	43,406.0
1894	67	73,359.3	41,979.8
1895	73	73,234.9	43,732.9
1896	106	92,321.9	54,551.7
1897	183	142,703.6	84,707.4
1898	237	176,820.7	120,788.3
1899	277	194,222.9	136,154.7
1900	279	189,316.3	142,703.2
1901	261	166,437.7	123,256.8
1902	241	152,391.9	113,313.0
1903	228	149,643.1	115,258.0
1904	209	141,430.3	108,951.3
1905	199	139,859.0	107,176.4
1906	204	146,021.1	111,097.0
1907	202	143,739.2	108,447.0
1908	194	152,677.6	116,155.7
1909	195	153,500.8	117,265.8
1910	204	167,670.9	120,770.0
1911	254	210,375.6	138,619.9
1912	279	257,518.8	181,940.2
1913	287	268,052.7	191,516.2
1914	288	281,295.6	200,686.0

failed. This was unlike the experience of Australia which had some success in floating a similar venture.[13]

Of the six other British direct investments in financial concerns, five companies centred their activities on the extension of mortgage loans. They were concentrated in the areas of early western expansion and their growth was linked directly to the expansion of the land companies, particularly in Manitoba. The other investment, the Trust and Loan Company of Canada, operated on a national scale and was also active in the extension of mortgage loans.

13 Breckenridge, p. 298

TABLE 3.4
Percentage distribution of the stock of British direct investment between sectors of the Canadian economy, selected years, 1890–1914

	Paid-up capital											
	1890		1895		1900		1905		1910		1914	
Sectors	%	Rank	%	Rank	%	Rank	%	Rank	%	Rank	%	Rank
(1)	(2)	(3)	(4)	(5)	(6)	(7)	(8)	(9)	(10)	(11)	(12)	(13)
Mining	18.0	6	19.5	3	64.7	1	55.0	1	33.3	1	27.3	1
Oil	4.6	4	7.3	5	3.3	6	1.7	6	3.6	6	1.6	7
Land	40.7	1	26.6	2	8.2	4	9.2	3	14.2	3	18.1	3
Timber	0.6	7	0.6	7	0.5	7	0.4	7	2.0	7	1.8	6
Finance	29.8	2	31.0	1	10.1	2	8.8	4	13.6	4	14.5	4
Distribution	—		—		0.1	8	0.3	8	0.2	8	0.2	8
Utilities	1.8	6	1.7	6	9.2	3	19.1	2	19.5	2	13.7	5
Manufacturing	4.4	5	13.2	4	6.4	5	5.9	5	13.5	5	22.9	2
TOTAL	100.0		100.0		100.0		100.0		100.0		100.0	
$ 000's	42,981		43,733		142,703		107,176		120,770		200,686	

AGGREGATE

Between 1889 and 1914 the total number of existing British direct investments in Canada increased from 64 to 288; the stock of investment increased fivefold. Jointly determined by the pattern of new investment and the withdrawal of British business enterprise, the stock of investment increased rapidly in the periods 1895-99 and 1910-14 (Table 3.3). The pattern traced by the stock of British direct investment confirms the growing importance of mining ventures (Table 3.4). Although land and financial investments formed the largest elements in 1890, as aggregate British investment grew, their funds in these sectors of the Canadian economy remained stable until 1906. The massive increases in the stock of investment in the mining sector in the period from 1895 to 1899 established the dominance of this part of the economy, in terms of British involvement, in the early twentieth century. Yet, when the total stock of British direct investment in Canada increased during the 'wheat boom' era, it was more widely distributed and evenly distributed by sector than in earlier years. In the manufacturing sector few British companies established branch plants in Canada, and it was in this area particularly that British direct investment fell far behind its American equivalent.

The lack of British investment in branch plants in the manufacturing sector helped to dictate the geographic location of the aggregate stock of British direct investment in Canada (Table 3.5). (Location is defined by the province in which the company was required to register. A company that carried on business in more than one province is classified as 'unassigned.') The stock of British direct investment located exclusively in Ontario and Quebec never exceeded 16.3 per cent. On the other hand, in 1900, 59.4 per cent of this investment was located west of the Manitoba-Ontario boundary, not counting the many firms classified as 'unassigned,' whose activities were restricted to western Canada. This geographic pattern of investment was determined by the large investment in the resource based sectors (mining, land, timber). Even in the finance and utilities and service sectors the British direct investments tended to concentrate their activities in the regions where the natural resource industries dominated. For the entire period 1890-1914, western Canada held the greatest attraction for British direct investment. However, it must be noted again that there is no evidence to suggest that western Canada had some inherent appeal to British entrepreneurs. Rather, British

TABLE 3.5
Percentage distribution of the stock of British direct investment between Canadian provinces, selected years, 1890–1914

Provinces	Paid-up capital											
	1890		1895		1900		1905		1910		1914	
	%	Rank	%	Rank	%	Rank	%	Rank	%	Rank	%	Rank
(1)	(2)	(3)	(4)	(5)	(6)	(7)	(8)	(9)	(10)	(11)	(12)	(13)
British Columbia	16.7	2	27.2	2	56.4	1	50.5	1	38.3	1	26.0	2
Alberta	1.7	7	1.0	8	0.4	10	4.4	5	7.8	4	8.8	4
Saskatchewan	1.5	8	2.3	7	0.7	8	0.3	10	1.0	9	0.9	9
Manitoba	5.5	5	6.6	6	1.9	7	2.4	8	2.4	7	1.7	7
Ontario	9.1	3	10.2	4	10.4	3	9.7	4	11.4	3	15.2	3
Quebec	4.2	6	5.1	5	5.3	5	2.4	7	1.8	8	1.1	8
Nova Scotia	7.8	4	11.1	3	2.8	6	3.8	6	4.2	5	2.0	6
New Brunswick	—		—		0.4	9	1.1	9	0.9	10	0.4	10
P.E.I.	—		—		—		—		—		—	
Yukon	—		—		9.3	4	10.3	3	3.8	6	4.3	5
Canada, unassigned	53.5	1	36.4	1	12.7	2	15.3	2	29.2	2	39.6	1
TOTAL	100.0		100.0		100.0		100.0		100.0		100.0	
$ 000's	42,981		43,733		142,703		107,176		120,770		200,686	

TABLE 3.6
Comparison of the stocks of British and United States direct investment in Canada for the year 1897

British			American (Lewis)		
Sector	Amount ($ m)	%	Sector	Amount ($ m)	%
(1)	(2)	(3)	(4)	(5)	(6)
Mining	45.7	54.1	Metals & minerals	55.0	34.5
Oil	3.2	3.7	Oil	6.0	4.0
Land	11.0	13.1	Agricultural	18.0	11.5
Timber	0.5	0.5	(see below)	—	—
Financial	13.8	16.3	—	—	—
Distribution	0.1	0.1	Selling orgns.	10.0	6.5
Utilities	2.3	2.7	Utilities & misc.	3.0	1.6
Manufacturing	7.8	9.4	Manufacturing (incl. pulp and paper)	55.0	34.5
—	—	—	Railroads	12.7	8.0
TOTAL	84.5	100.0	TOTAL	159.7	100.0

SOURCE: Lewis, 575

direct investments were located in this region largely because of the type of activity they preferred to undertake.

Since the stock of British direct investment in Canada is calculated on a yearly basis for the entire period 1890-1914, certain comparisons can be made. First, these data can be compared with those collected on American direct investment in Canada for the years 1897, 1909, and 1913 in order to determine if British and American investments of this type were of comparable size and distributed within the Canadian economy in a similar manner. Second, the data presented in this study can be compared with Field's estimates of British 'miscellaneous investments in Canada' for the years immediately preceding World War I. A comparison with Field's data is critical, since they are the only independent estimates of 'British direct investment' in Canada which present an aggregate and distribution of this aggregate among various sectors of the Canadian economy.

Data on American direct investment in Canada were collected for the year 1897 using the same criteria as used here. It was shown that in 1897 there was a total United States financial stock of direct investment of 159.7 million (Table 3.6). Because of the omission from this study of British direct investment in railroads, the American total must be deflated by 8 per cent to make the estimates comparable. Although both totals are large, British direct investment in Canada was only 57.5 per cent of the comparable American investment. However, the discrepancy between the totals was due almost entirely to the existence of branch plants of American firms in Canadian manufacturing. This had always been a major sector of American activity because of the need to jump the Canadian tariff wall.[14] When this special sphere of American influence is omitted from consideration, British direct investment in 1897 was 91.0 per cent of the American stock. Unfortunately, the American data restrict comparisons since it may be argued that the year 1897 is a singularly inappropriate year to measure the stock of British direct investment in Canada. It increased to $120.6 million in 1898 and to $142.5 million in 1900, and it is likely that peaks in the stock of American direct investment preceded the peaks in its British equivalent, if supply conditions were of importance, because of the close association between the Canadian and American business cycles.[15]

Apart from the distribution of British and American direct investment, and from that in the manufacturing sector, the pattern is broadly similar. In the mining, oil, land (agricultural enterprises), and utilities and service sectors of the Canadian economy the stock of American direct investment was only slightly greater than that of the British. On the other hand, there was a large American investment in the Canadian distributive sector that was not matched by any similar British involvement.[16] In the Canadian financial sector there was no American direct investment, but a large amount of British activity. Thus, apart from the American investment in branch plants in Canada, the American did not overshadow the British direct investment in Canada in 1897. Similarly for the years 1909 and 1913, American direct investment in Canada dominates its British counterpart by its manufacturing component. The American estimates are not as precise as those for the year 1897 and only very rough comparisons can be

14 Buckley, 66. M. Wilkins, *The emergence of multinational enterprise* (Cambridge, Mass., 1970), pp. 135-48

15 Chambers, 406

16 Although there is no guiding evidence, this difference may simply be a reflection of the different types of business organizations used as distributive agencies for British and American manufacturing firms. As noted, British manufacturers did not create separate firms or subsidiary organizations to market their products in Canada.

TABLE 3.7
Stock of United States direct investment in Canada, 1909 and 1913

Sector	1909		1913	
	$ m	%	$ m	%
(1)	(2)	(3)	(4)	(5)
Branch companies	105.0	41.4	135.0	30.4
Packing plants	5.0	2.0	6.8	1.5
British Columbian lumber, timber and paper mills	58.0	22.8	71.0	16.0
British Columbian mines	50.0	19.7	62.0	13.9
Land deals in British Columbia	4.5	1.8	60.0	13.5
Land deals in Prairies	20.0	7.9	41.0	9.2
City and town property	—	—	20.0	4.5
Others	11.6	5.0	49.6	11.2
TOTAL	254.1	100.0	445.4	100.0

SOURCE: Field (1911), 24 and Field (1914), 25

made.[17] They do, nevertheless, confirm that United States direct investment was by the end of the period 1890–1914 substantially greater than British direct investment, $445.4 million and $191.5 million respectively in 1913. Again, as in 1897, the American dominance appears to have been restricted exclusively to the investment in branch plants and in the lumber and pulp and paper industry (Table 3.7). Pulp and paper was not an industry that attracted much British attention.

As noted earlier, there exists a set of estimates of British investments in Canada for the period 1909–13 that can be used in comparison with the estimates presented in this study (Table 3.8). (Field's estimates are presented in Table 1.1.) It can be seen that these estimates correspond very closely to those presented here and as the only independent data on the stock of British direct investment in Canada they support the aggregate figures presented in this study (Table 3.9). Field's estimates (calculated in 1914) appear to under-

17 I suspect that Field's figures on American investment are not nearly as reliable as his figures on British investment. The identification of American firms investing in Canada would not normally be as easy (on registration) as the identification of British firms. His figures also, most probably, include estimates of private holdings of Americans in Canada.

TABLE 3.8
Estimates of the stock of British direct investment in Canada, selected years, 1909-1913 ($000's)

Year		Field's estimates
(1)	(2)	(3)
1909	117,266	103,535
1911	138,619	135,180
1913	191,516	171,000

SOURCE: Tables 1.1 and 3.3

TABLE 3.9
Comparison of estimates of British direct investment in the sectors of the Canadian economy, selected years 1909-1913 ($ m)

				Field's estimates		
Sector	1909	1911	1913	1909	1911	1913
(1)	(2)	(3)	(4)	(5)	(6)	(7)
Mining	45.9	40.9	43.9	56.3	57.6	59.0
Land (and lumber purchases)	15.4	21.7	37.1	19.0	42.5	65.0
Financial	9.9	25.9	29.7	5.7	8.7	12.0
Manufacturing (industrial)	15.6	18.0	46.2	22.5	26.4	35.0

( ) denote Field's categories.

SOURCE: Table 1.1

estimate slightly the stock of British direct investment in Canada during this period. There are some significant differences between the compositions of the two estimates. Field, for example, estimated too highly the extent of British direct investment in the Canadian mining sector. It is likely that he did not have completely accurate information on (i) some early registrations and (ii) failures of mining companies. However, Field's estimates do imply that the extent of investment in mining was not growing as quickly as the investment in other sectors, and, in that sense, concur with the conclusions presented here. Unfortunately, Field's figures give no indication of the long down swing in the level of British direct investment in mining from 1900 to 1912.

The estimates calculated in this study imply that Field grossly overestimated the British direct investment in land and grossly underestimated the investment in financial concerns. Curiously, if the stocks of investment are summed for the land and financial sectors in each case, the results compare favourably. It is possible that Field classified many financial companies whose activities were related to the land sector as land companies or urban real estate companies. (His system of classification is not revealed.) It is also possible that he attempted to adjust his estimate of the investment in land to account for Canadian land held by private individuals in the United Kingdom. This, however, would leave unexplained the underestimate of the stock of British direct investment in the Canadian financial sector. Thus, in 1912, land investment was not in fact the most important area of British direct investment in Canada as indicated at the time by Field.

It is clear from the comparisons made above that many important features of stock of British direct investment in Canada are masked by an examination of the aggregates. Subsequent sections of this chapter will examine the disaggregated sectoral distribution of British business activity.

MINING*

The paid-up capital of the active British mining companies in Canada in 1890 totalled $7,598,000. In the following two years the stock of investment rose and reached a high point for the quinquennium in 1892. By 1895 phosphate production in Quebec had become spasmodic because of the low prices that followed the discovery of large natural phosphate deposits in the United States; total Canadian production in that year of 1,822 tons was less than six per cent of the 1890 output.[18] With the decline in the high price for phosphate in these years many firms incurred heavy losses.[19] Among the firms forced out of business were two British companies, the Canadian Phosphate Company Limited and the General Phosphate Company Limited. Along with these companies many of the small existing mining companies also failed. Consequently, there were fewer British mining companies in Canada at the beginning of 1895 than there were in 1890.

* For sectoral estimates of the stock of British direct investment in Canada see Appendix B.

18 *Annual Report on Mineral Production, 1909*, 281

19 *The Canadian Mining and Mechanical Review*, February 1894, 21

The next five years saw a growth in the stock of investment associated with the mining booms in British Columbia and the Yukon. In 1900 the peak stock of investment $92,174,000 was reached. This represented approximately 77.5 per cent of the level of nominal capital. By 1900, Nova Scotia had ceased to be a dominant mining area in the distribution of British mining investment as the marginally profitable gold mines of that province succumbed to the competition of the newer precious metal discoveries. In all parts of Canada the increases in the stock of investment were almost solely a result of the increases in the investments in gold and non-ferrous metal production.

After the peak in 1900, the stock of British direct investment in Canadian mining declined every year to 1910. At first this rapid decline (1900-2) was the result of the great number of liquidations of hastily formed companies registered in the immediate pre-1900 period, but throughout the decade British mining ventures steadily withdrew from Canada. Despite the growing value of mineral production in British Columbia, the faster growing value of mineral production in Ontario did not induce a switch in the geographic proportions of the stock of British mining investment. As noted earlier, the decade 1900-9 was one in which general subscriptions of mining capital fell in the British market, reaching a low in 1908,[20] and this low level of company formation reflected itself in the number of companies active in Canada at this time.

Except in 1912, the stock of British direct investment in Canadian mining increased in every year between 1909 and 1915. By 1914 Ontario accounted for 44.6 per cent of British business activity in this sector. Mining in Alberta and Saskatchewan had received injections of British capital since 1900, and in 1914 these provinces held about 8.2 per cent of the $54,321,000 total. A renewed interest in the Klondyke area increased, at least temporarily, the stock of British direct investment in the Yukon. Nova Scotia, the major host area in 1890, held no major British mining investments in 1914.

It is apparent that the geographic distribution of the stock of British direct investment in Canadian mining broadly resembled the relative geographic distribution of total mineral output. For British Columbia this is evident in Table 3.10. To the extent that British investment did not exactly follow the distribution of output, explanation can be sought in (i) the absence of British direct investment in

20 Jackson, p. 166

TABLE 3.10
Distribution by type of the mineral output of British Columbia, selected years (% of mining output, current prices)

Type	1890	1895	1900	1902
(1)	(2)	(3)	(4)	(5)
Gold: placer	18.8	8.5	7.8	6.1
lode	nil	13.9	21.1	28.0
Silver	2.8	17.3	14.1	11.1
Copper	nil	0.8	9.9	19.7
Lead	nil	9.4	16.5	4.7
Coal	78.0	50.0	26.4	24.0
Coke	nil	0.1	2.6	3.6
Others	0.4	—	1.5	2.7
TOTAL	100.0	100.0	100.0	100.0
(Total value)	($2,608,803)	($5,643,042)	($16,344,751)	($17,486,650)

SOURCE: Mineral Production of British Columbia (1902), 16 (1905), 17

non-metallic minerals and (ii) the slower reaction to the discovery of new mineral producing areas than that of domestic or United States investors. The production of non-metallic minerals increased absolutely from 1890 to 1914, but their relative significance to total mineral output declined from 40.0 to 25.9 per cent. With the notable exceptions of asbestos, mica, and phosphate, the majority of non-metallic minerals were sold only in the domestic market. This sector did not grow at the rate of those mining sectors whose growth in output was export-led and attracted virtually no British direct investment. Consequently, the rising value of mineral output in Quebec (almost entirely confined to non-metallic minerals) was not incompatible with small stocks of British mining capital in that area. Second, the stock of British direct investment in non-ferrous metals and gold and silver in Ontario lagged significantly behind the quantitative significance of these sectors. Although British Columbia had ceased to be 'The Mineral Province' in 1907 when the value of mining output in Ontario surpassed it, the stock of British investment in Ontario did not reflect this change until 1912.[21] (There is also evidence, which will be considered later, which suggests that British investment in the west prior to 1900 also lagged behind the changing distribution of total industrial investment.) It was during the period 1910–14 that

21 *Annual Report on Mineral Production* (1914), 38

TABLE 3.11
Distribution of Canadian mineral output by area and type, selected years, 1890–1914

Area	1890		1900		1910		1914	
	$ 000's	%	$ 000's	%	$ 000's	%	$ 000's	%
(1)	(2)	(3)	(4)	(5)	(6)	(7)	(8)	(9)
Nova Scotia	4,146	24.7	6,298	9.8	14,196	13.3	17,585	13.7
British Columbia	2,704	16.1	16,681	25.9	24,479	22.9	24,164	18.8
Ontario	2,958[a]	17.6	11,258	17.5	43,538	40.8	53,035	41.0
Quebec	3,070	18.3	3,292	5.1	8,270	7.7	11,838	9.2
Manitoba	15				1,500	1.4	2,413	1.9
Saskatchewan	10	2.4	1,089	1.7	498	0.5	712	0.6
Alberta	202				8,996	8.4	12,682[a]	9.8
Yukon	175		22,453	34.9	4,764	4.5	5,418	4.2
Unclassified and misc. production (incl. petroleum)	3,483	20.8	3,350	5.2	582	0.5	1,016	0.8
TOTALS	16,763	100.0	64,421	100.0	106,823	100.0	128,863	100.0
Type								
Metallic minerals (excl. gold)	2,344	14.0	11,955	18.6	37,354	35.0	42,173	32.7
Gold	1,150	6.9	27,908	43.3	10,206	9.6	15,983	12.4
Non-metallic minerals	6,690	40.0	9,248	14.4	27,338	25.6	33,407	25.9
Fuels (coal)	5,676	33.9	13,742	21.3	30,910	28.9	33,472	26.0
Misc. (incl. petroleum)	903	5.4	1,568	5.2	1,735	1.6	3,828	3.0
TOTALS	16,763	100.0	64,421	100.0	106,823	100.0	128,863	100.0

[a]Excluding petroleum

SOURCES: *The Annual Report on the Mineral Production of Canada during the Calendar Year, 1914*, Department of Mines (Ottawa, 1915), 33; *The Canada Yearbook*, 1915 (Ottawa, 1916), 239; 'Historical summary of Canada's mineral production,' *Annual Report on Mineral Production, 1944*, 29–34

British direct investment in Canadian mining adjusted to the changed focus of the Canadian mining industry. Only then did the absolute and relative levels of this investment in Ontario conform to the structure of mineral outputs.

Throughout the period 1890–1914 British direct investments were concentrated in the metallic mining and fuel mining industries of the Canadian mining sector. Especially after 1895, a relatively high and stable proportion of this investment was engaged in non-ferrous metallic mining. This proportion averaged between 50 and 60 per cent. It was a reflection of the growing importance of non-ferrous metallic mining to total industry output, evident in Table 3.11. The stock of British direct investment in the British Columbia mining sector conformed very closely to the structure of mining output. Here non-metallic minerals, excluding fuel, were not an important contribution to the value of mineral production. The proportion of the stock of British direct investment in gold mining operation was 5.3 per cent, reflecting the absolutely low level of gold production in Canada in 1890, when only 56,000 troy ounces of gold were produced. Peak gold production for the 1890–1914 period was recorded ten years later, in 1900, when the Klondyke output swelled aggregate Canadian production to 1.35 million troy ounces.[22] British investment in gold mining in this year reached $36,554,000. Although the absolute investment in gold mining waned, the proportion of gold mining activities to all other sectors remained high, 21.1 per cent in 1910 and 30.6 per cent in 1914. Prior mention has been made of British investments in Canadian coal mines. The relative importance of this sector to the British investor declined as the new mineral sectors grew. However, coal mining did provide a not inconsiderable outlet for investment funds in a growing domestic market.

In summary, the stock of British direct investment in the Canadian mining sector increased most rapidly during the period 1895–9. The overall stock of this investment, however, decreased for most of the period 1900–13 despite the high real growth rates achieved in the production of non-ferrous metals. This was a consequence of the failure of a large number of firms created by the earlier boom. The high incidence of these mining failures more than offset the increased new investment after 1906. As a consequence, the stock of British direct investment in the Canadian mining industry never achieved a level comparable to the peak of the British Columbia-Yukon mining boom.

22 Urquhart and Buckley, p. 412

Part of the explanation for this decline in the stock of investment over the period 1900–13 can be found in the unfavourable profitability record of British mining investments in Canada.

OIL

Canada during the period 1890–1914 was one of many minor oil producing nations. The stock of British direct investment reflected the modest level of oil production and at no time exceeded $5 million. Most of the British business activity was centred on the Ontario oil fields and this investment was concentrated in the exploration for oil and simple refining. Many companies' main assets were not the physical capital of oil rigs and refineries. For instance, in 1907 the Anglo-Canadian Petroleum Company Limited held 21 separate oil leases in the oil producing counties of western Ontario. At cost price these leases were valued at approximately $305 thousand. On the other hand, the physical capital of the company, which consisted of well equipment, was valued at only $20 thousand.[23] Most of the British companies were small and closely resembled the more speculative sections of the mining sector, with a low ratio of cash subscriptions to issued shares and few fixed interest securities.

It is worth noting that many of the companies involved in this sector were founded in the years of a worldwide oil boom. Thirteen of the twenty-eight new British direct investments in the Canadian oil sector were formed during a period of intense British interest in the oil fields at Maikop in the South Caucasus of Russia. The boom which lasted from about 1908 to 1912 was also sustained by British involvement in the oil fields in Burma.[24] This was the first major oil boom experienced by British investors. Many of the firms formed to invest in this boom had direct ties with those formed to invest in Canadian oil. The Anglo-Canadian Petroleum Company Limited, which became active in Ontario, was initially formed and promoted by the Roumanian Development Syndicate Limited.[25] Similar ties existed between

23 The company's equipment and plant consisted of: 7 pumping rigs, 1 20-H.P. Boiler, 1 20-H.P. gas engine, 1 20-H.P. Steam Engine, piping, tubing, and some small storage tanks. This well illustrates the small scale of the physical investment in capital. The Anglo-Canadian Petroleum Company Limited, *P.R.O.*, 90537/BT/31/11694

24 *The Oil, Petroleum and Bitumen Manual, 1910*, ed. W.S. Skinner (London, 1910), 4. This was the first edition of any major directory to inform British investors about British oil companies.

25 The Anglo-Canadian Petroleum Company Limited, *P.R.O.*, 90537/BT/31/11694

other companies.[26] Many directors of the British companies involved in Canada also sat on the boards of some of the large companies investing in Russia.[27] Although the evidence is not overwhelming, it does suggest that the new British direct investment in Canadian oil was solely a result of 'push' factors. That is, the new investment was a reaction, a type of echo phenomenon, to the intense interest in oil elsewhere. This kind of 'spillover' investment was not confined to Canada but was found in many of the world's small but active oil fields in New Zealand, Peru, Trinidad, and British North Borneo.[28]

TIMBER

The growth of the pulp and paper industries in eastern Canada was the principal characteristic of the forest industries in the twenty-five years prior to 1914. The gross value of pulp and paper and its products rose from $4 million in 1890 to $21 million in 1900, and to $47 million in 1910. Between 1890 and 1900 this was almost entirely a real increase, although in the subsequent decade price increases accounted for 43 per cent of the increased value. The real and price increases were largely a response to a growing export demand for these products in the United States. (By 1930, newsprint paper was Canada's second leading export commodity.)[29]

One of the British investments in the province of New Brunswick engaged in the production of pulp and paper after acquiring an existing Canadian pulp mill in 1897. However, although the company operated for twenty-three years, it was seldom out of financial difficulty.[30] This was the only major new British direct investment in the eastern Canadian forest industries. Nine British firms, however, operated in British Columbia's forest industry. These varied in type from companies that did little more than hold timber rights to companies that cut timber and operated saw mills. One sulphite pulp mill was owned consecutively by two British companies and the second, the

26 Canadian Oil Corporation Limited, *P.R.O.*, 136500/BT/31/32188; the Canada Petroleum Company Limited, *P.R.O.*, 61627/BT/31/3468; the Canadian Lubricating Oil Syndicate Limited, *P.R.O.*, 113178/BT/31/19769

27 For example, E.M. Bovill was a director of the Maikop European and General Oil Trust Limited, in addition to the Standard Oil Company of Canada Limited.

28 *The Oil Manual, 1912*, vi

29 Firestone, p. 213; Urquhart and Buckley, p. 294

30 The Dominion Pulp Company Limited, *P.R.O.*, 5266/BT/31/15783

Swanson Bay Forests, Wood Pulp and Lumber Mills Limited, was one of the few British direct investments with a separate Canadian charter and, therefore, the status of a British subsidiary in Canada.

A small cluster of new registrations occurred in the years from 1910 to 1912 when more nominal and paid-up capital was created for direct investment by the British in the Canadian forest industry than in any other period. This coincided with the renewed interest of the British capital market in the timber industries. The bulk of British savings were used, however, to buy the bonds of Canadian and American companies in Canada which supplied the American market, rather than to sponsor direct participation.[31]

LAND

With the collapse of the minor western Canadian land boom in the 1880s, Canadian agriculture and land expansion in the west was arrested. From 1890 to 1895, the agricultural sector was depressed, immigration into Canada remained low, and the process of western settlement was impeded. In 1896, the increase in the price of wheat in conjunction with falling shipping charges and the general stimulation of world demand induced by the additions to the world's gold stock and the resulting increase in production helped to stimulate a new era of agricultural expansion. The reduction in the exportable agricultural surplus of the United States and the final settlement of all unoccupied land in that country produced the impetus for a new period of growth in Canada. This period lasted from 1896 to 1913. The first few years, from 1896 to 1900, were years of recovery during which economic growth increased sharply in some sectors. The years from 1901 to 1913, with only a few exceptions, were characterized by the long sustained wheat boom when the entire economy shared in the prosperity. During this latter period Canada assimilated over one million immigrants in the west alone, increased the amount of land in productive agriculture from 63.4 million acres in 1901 to 109.0 million acres in 1911, increased merchandise exports from $183 million in 1900 to $380 million in 1913, and, as previously noted, absorbed vast imports of foreign capital. The 1901-13 boom was accompanied by rapid urban growth in both western and eastern Canada. The stock of British direct investment in the Canadian land and agricultural sector did not conform, however, to the tripartite

31 Field (1914), p. 138 and Lewis, pp. 295-7

period of depression, recovery, and boom. Net additions to the stock remained relatively constant until the zenith of the wheat boom period. Thus, from the point of view of British business activity in this sector, the period 1890-1914 is broken into two stages, one of relative inactivity, the other of intense activity in the process of new investment. This pattern is evident from the profile of new registrations. Not only were few new companies formed during the years 1890 to 1907 but no less than 16 of the existing companies found it necessary to reorganize their financial structures in order to remain active.

In Canada, from 1890 to approximately 1896, the total land sales of the Hudson's Bay Company and the railway companies were depressed in the face of relatively low land prices.[32] (In 1894, 68.7 thousand acres of land from this source were sold, compared with 648.4 thousand acres in 1900, and 4.2 million acres in 1902.)[33] In addition, there was a general lack of trading in large blocks of land which were being held by speculators in anticipation of rising prices.[34] Since many of the British direct investments themselves had to purchase land from speculators in the 1880s and later in the immediate pre-war years, there were few tracts of land being offered to British entrepreneurs. Furthermore, in 1896, the United Kingdom enforced a permanent embargo against the live importation of Canadian cattle into Britain. (A temporary embargo had been instituted in 1892.)[35] This finally eroded the traditional advantage of British direct investment in cattle ranching which consisted of facilities to fatten cattle after the trans-Atlantic crossing. Thus, the growing ranching industry, despite the increased shipment of cattle, failed to attract much new British direct investment. The only British company to invest solely in this industry between 1890 and 1907 shipped slaughtered meat to Britain.[36]

32 Throughout the entire period 1870-1914, the British press devoted many editorials to the dangers of investing in Canadian, Australian and other overseas land.
33 Urquhart and Buckley, p. 367
34 J. Long, *Canadian Agriculture, Report by Prof. James Long*, Department of the Interior (London, 1894), 8-9
35 Although live cattle could be imported under the embargo, they had to be slaughtered immediately. The embargo was in force until 1932. Murchie, p. 57. R. Wallace, *Special Report on the Agricultural Resources of Canada*, Department of the Interior (London, 1894), p. 25-8
36 The Maple Creek (Canada) Cattle Company Limited, *P.R.O.*, 53566/BT/31/15820

TABLE 3.12
Registration of new British direct investments
in the Canadian land sector and sub-divisions, 1890–1914

Period	Sub-divisions of land sector: Rural land	Urban land	Miscel-laneous land	Land and agriculture	Agriculture	Total
(1)	(2)	(3)	(4)	(5)	(6)	(7)
1890–1894	2	0	2	0	1	5
1895–1899	0	2	1	1	0	4
1900–1904	3	0	1	0	0	4
1905–1909	4	3	4	1	2	14
1910–1914	16	25	21	7	5	74

Despite the dramatic changes in 1896 in the nature of the demand for capital in Canadian agriculture, very little new direct investment in land was undertaken. Even after 1901 when the number of homestead entries and the total land sales of major land companies had increased over previous years,[37] there was no significant change in the pattern of British business participation in this sector despite the larger dividend payments being made by existing firms. Further increases in the price of land due to the diminution of the amount of free land available to settlers[38] also failed to encourage a response.

The end of a period of reduced British overseas lending in 1905 and the general fast pace of western expansion in Canada finally combined to produce renewed interest in 1906 (see Table 3.12). This expansion was most clearly evident to potential new investors in the large dividend payments being made by the existing British direct investments in western Canadian land. In that year over $7.5 million of nominal financial capital was registered by four new direct investing

37 'Annual Report of the Department of the Interior,' *Sessional Papers, 1915*, No. 25 (Ottawa, 1915), xx-xxvii

38 'Evidence of Mr. R.E. Young of the Department of the Interior,' *Evidence Heard Before a Select Committee of the Senate of Canada* (Ottawa, 1908), 27-9. One indication of the general trend of land prices is the change in the average price received by the Hudson's Bay Company and the railroad companies for land sold. This increase was 59.5 per cent between 1900 and 1905, but probably also reflects the desirability of prime land near railroads. Other agricultural land did not increase so greatly in price.

firms. Of these four companies, three became active in Alberta and one in British Columbia, and they acquired not only rural land but also coal rights, urban real estate, and fruit farms. The stock of direct investment then remained relatively unchanged during the short sharp depression of 1906 and the poor harvest year of 1907.[39] Interest was, however, again active by 1908. Land prices, both rural and urban, continued to rise at an ever faster pace than prior to 1907, about 10 per cent in Manitoba and 30 per cent in Alberta and Saskatchewan in the following five years.[40] As land prices increased more large blocks of land were released by speculators and much of this in turn was bought by new land companies in the anticipation of even greater price rises.

Typically the British firms dealing in rural land were located in western Canada. Large blocks of land were acquired, subdivided, and resold. On occasion improvements might be undertaken to enhance the value of the company's land holding. For instance, the Southern Alberta Land Company Limited, founded in 1906, issued over $1 million 5 and 6 per cent debenture stock to finance a vast irrigation project covering 200 thousand acres of the company's land.[41] Improvements were made by all British firms promoting fruit growing land in British Columbia. The value of this land largely lay in its being well cultivated and irrigated. Often, the sales of land were carried on along with a genuine farming activity on the part of the firm, and it was not unusual that land sold to individuals already contained mature fruit plants. (The most popular fruits were apples, peaches, and pears.) Without fruit plants but with improvements and irrigation, blocks of land were selling as early as 1907 for approximately $140 to $200 per acre.[42] Thus, the initial holdings of this type of British direct investment in land were usually much smaller than

39 A.K. Cairncross, 'Investment in Canada, 1900-1913,' *The export of capital from Britain, 1870-1914*, ed. A.R. Hall (London, 1968), p. 168

40 *The Economist*, 9 March 1912, 515; O.J. Firestone, *Canada's economic development, 1867-1953*, Income and Wealth Series VII (London, 1958), p. 86

41 *Canadian Industrial and Misc. Companies*, 77-8; *The Stock Exchange Year-Book, 1915*, 827-8

42 J.M. Gibbon, 'The Scot in Canada,' *Aberdeen Daily Journal* (Aberdeen, 1907), 10-11. The prices of prairie land in contrast could be represented by those charged by one major British land company.

1901	$2.96	1908	$8.60
1903	$4.12	1914	$9.36
1907	$8.21	1915	$9.00

those holding cereal land, because of the high purchase price that had to be paid by the company or the large amount of development expenditure required. The Nicola Valley Land and Trust Company Limited purchased only 3,760 acres of fruit land in British Columbia in 1912 for $117,419 with the expectation of being able to resell the land at a minimum of $194 per acre.[43]

Although the British urban real estate firms were geographically more widespread, the majority did tend to concentrate in the newer urban areas of western Canada. The major urban centres of Montreal, Toronto, and Hamilton did attract some investment, but not as much as Victoria, Vancouver, Calgary, Winnipeg, and other newer urban areas.[44] Some of these companies investing in urban real estate did improve the sites. Drainage was provided and in some cases houses were built and the land sold fully developed.[45] However, the majority of British direct investments in urban real estate did not undertake improvements irrespective of whether they bought developed sites with buildings or undeveloped town property. As illustrated below, the firms that undertook investment activity tended to concentrate their assets in western Canada as evident in the case of Western Canada Townlots in Table 3.13. The preponderance of urban real estate investment in the west was solidly based on the faster urban growth in that region and the greater demand for houses,[46] which caused the price of urban real estate to rise faster there. Throughout the period 1908–13 these rising prices encouraged further British direct investment in Canadian real estate.[47]

By late 1913 the boom in both rural and urban real estate was over. It had been brought to an end by the more restrictive loan and

43 Prospectus, Nicola Valley Land and Trust Company Limited, *S.C.R.O.*, 8415 Diss.

44 The major British direct investment in land in Toronto noted by Field (1914), p. 141 was confirmed. The company was the Toronto and Canadian Lands Limited. No other purchases of land in Toronto, Montreal, or Hamilton of this size (250 acres for $500,000) were recorded. Toronto and Canadian Lands Limited, *P.R.O.*, 127055/BT/31/21220

45 For example in Calgary and Port Arthur, Ontario, the following British direct investments built dwellings: The Dominion Building Company Limited, *P.R.O.*, 129087/BT/31/21470; The Port Arthur (Ontario) Buildings Limited, *P.R.O.*, 13400/BT/31/22065.

46 Cairncross, p. 154

47 Field (1914), p. 140. 'The rapid appreciation of real estate values in or near growing towns, large and small, is becoming a matter of more common knowledge across the ocean.'

TABLE 3.13
Physical assets of Western Canada Townlots Limited, 1913

Asset		Value at cost ($)
Regina, Sask.	316 acres	56,949
Saskatoon, Sask.	160 acres	55,867
Yorkton, Sask.	77 acres	31,942
Winnipeg, Man.	103 lots	2,731
Cromdale, Man.	4 lots	922
Fort William, Ont.	100 lots	14,069
South Vancouver, B.C.	56 lots	8,594
Saint John, N.B.	110 acres	73,250
Misc.		26,001
TOTAL		270,324

Balance Sheet, 31 July 1914, Western Canada Townlots Limited, *P.R.O.*, 115853/BT/31/20017

mortgage policies of financial companies in Canada. The real estate mania ended and many of the more speculative ventures were forced into liquidation.

FINANCE

During the period 1890–1914, fifty new British direct investments became active in the Canadian financial sector. Of these, twenty-one were formed directly as mortgage companies or trust and loan companies involved in mortgage extensions. The other twenty-nine companies were formed for the purposes of general investment in Canada, but many centred much of their activities in the mortgage and loan field and the promotion of land settlement. Of these fifty companies only two restricted their area of operation to eastern Canada. All the others were either exclusively or mainly active in western Canada. In western Canada not only was the process of agricultural expansion greater than in the older regions of the country, but the rate of urbanization was also greater and this in turn created a demand for home mortgages.[48] However, the majority of firms were in the busi-

48 I.A. Anderson, *Internal migration in Canada, 1921–1961*, Staff Study No. 13, Economic Council of Canada (Ottawa, 1966), p. 10

ness of the extension of farm mortgages. The popularity of this type of investment was founded on the very high proportion of owner-occupied farms. In Saskatchewan in 1901, 96.1 per cent of the farm land in production was owned by the occupiers.[49] This was a result of the government's free land policy, which restricted the amount of land one individual could take up and of the tendency of farmers to sell their holdings and move to cheap land when the price of farm land rose, thus stimulating the demand for farm mortgages.[50]

The collapse of the western Canadian land boom in the late 1880s did not immediately bring about the collapse of the demand for farm mortgages. At this time the majority of British direct investments involved in financing mortgages were located in the older regions of prairie settlement, especially Manitoba, an area affected less than the frontier by the end of the land boom. As noted earlier, the failure of the land boom lay in the failure of prices to rise and not in the collapse of rising land prices. In the early 1890s, as throughout the period 1890–1914, there was seldom a direct connection between land companies and mortgage and loan companies. In the areas where British direct investments had extended mortgages in the 1880s there was no dramatic collapse in the price of land and, although the rate of mortgage extension was not high, there were still profitable opportunities for financial companies in the west (see the dividend streams of the financial companies in Table 2.6).

After 1890, however, there was a slowing down in the rate of mortgage extension. The total mortgage loans extended by all loan companies and building societies increased from $108.8 million in 1890 to only $113.7 million in 1892.[51] Decreases in new investment in British financial companies in Canada after 1890 were not simply a reaction to the collapse of the land boom. Low agricultural prices and the generally depressed state of agriculture in the early 1890s did lead to a lower demand for mortgages in the prairie region and thus fewer new companies were interested in the Canadian financial sector at this time.[52]

The long period from 1893 to 1905 saw few new British direct investments in this area and very little new investment by existing

49 G.E. Britnell, *The wheat economy* (Toronto, 1939), p. 45

50 *The Economist*, 16 March 1912, 573

51 'Annual Report,' *S.P.* No. 10C, 42

52 The export price index of Canadian agricultural products (foods) declined every year from 1891 to 1895. In 1891 it was 118.0, falling to 90.3 in 1895 (1900 = 100). Urquhart and Buckley, p. 299

financial companies. The lack of attractive terms for agricultural mortgages was determined first by the depressed state of agriculture prior to the price changes in the late 1890s and then by the vast amounts of free and cheap land taken up after 1900. There appears to be a lag between the taking up of frontier land and the demand for mortgages in previously farmed areas. (It is possible that later immigrants to the prairies, because they had capital, preferred cultivated farms.) It was not until 1906 that the new influx of British direct investments in financial concerns materialized. The general unattractiveness of mortgage investment between 1893 and 1905 is pointed up by the portfolio selection of the British life insurance companies in Canada. (Canadian law required that British insurance companies operating in Canada hold Canadian assets equal to the amount of Canadian liabilities.) Mortgage loans on all types of real estate held by all British life insurance companies remained almost constant between 1894 and 1906 despite a general growth in assets from $19.3 million to $24.5 million.[53]

It was not until mortgage rates had risen to new high levels that new British direct investment was renewed. Rates of return on mortgages, after 1906, could be as high as 8 per cent.[54] Yet, the three years from 1906 to 1909 were marked by cautious optimism and it was not until 1910 that the surge of new investment took place.[55] This new investment was largely a response to the growing amount of dividends issued by existing British direct investments in Canada's financial sector, which itself was a symptom of increasing demand for mortgages as the amount of free land available to settlers rapidly diminished and as the amount of land released by the land companies for private sale increased. The growth in the demand for mortgages, and the willingness of British direct investments to supply them, are well illustrated by the growth of the value of mortgages in the balance sheets of the three companies mentioned below (Table 3.14). Only

53 Urquhart and Buckley, p. 256

54 'Report of Paper Read to the Institute of Actuaries, Canada by A.D. Besant,' *The Economist*, 26 Dec. 1914, 1099

55 The yield on city mortgages (1900 = 100) remained relatively stable until 1905. The yields increased most rapidly after 1910 despite the sudden increase in 1907.

1905	99.7	1908	106.1	1911	111.0
1906	102.5	1909	107.2	1912	114.7
1907	108.6	1910	109.8	1913	121.2

Cited in Cairncross, p. 185

TABLE 3.14
Mortgage assets of three British direct investments in the Canadian financial sector, selected years, 1908-1915 ($'s at face value)

Year	North of Scotland Canadian Mortgage Co. Ltd.*	British Canadian Trust Ltd.	Canada North Western Investment Co. Ltd.
(1)	(2)	(3)	(4)
1908	4,908,632	—	—
1911	—	839,186	—
1912	6,893,286	1,410,986	—
1913	—	1,802,289	53,568
1914	8,293,752	1,940,034	103,906
1915	—	1,922,724	—

*Less provision for contingencies

SOURCES: North of Scotland Canadian Mortgage Company Limited, *S.C.R.O.*, 642; British Canadian Trust Limited, *S.C.R.O.*, 7466; Canada North Western Investment Company Limited, *S.C.R.O.*, 8204 Diss., selected balance sheets

the North of Scotland Canadian Mortgage Company Limited was an established investment prior to 1890, whereas the British Canadian Trust Limited was formed in 1910 and the Canada North Western Investment Company Limited was formed in 1912.

The course of new British direct investment in Canadian finance continued at a high level until 1913 although the peak of this new investment had been reached in 1911. However, in late 1913 there was a sharp change in the willingness to invest in the Canadian financial sector. This became evident in 1914. In reaction to a fall in the price of Canada's wheat exports in 1912/13,[56] the existing mortgage companies in Canada became extremely cautious in evaluating the securities offered by their customers and slightly less interested in a high rate of return. High rates of return had often meant accepting risky securities on mortgages. The mortgage and loan companies acted in advance of any substantial fall in land prices.[57] Clearly evident by the beginning of 1913 is the action of the mortgage companies acting as a brake on the land market by attempting to offset the

56 Easterbrook and Aitken, p. 486

57 *The Economist*, 11 July 1914, 59. 'City men and investors generally, ... are so deeply interested in Canada that they naturally watch very closely all indications that are forthcoming as to the width and depth of the present depression.'

land price inflation which increasingly was being viewed as unstable.[58] This prevalent attitude was confirmed by the Canadian banks which, after January 1913, became very reluctant to supply advances for speculative purposes in the bull market for Canadian land.[59]

In summary, the decreases in new British direct investment in the Canadian financial sector in the periods 1890-93 and 1912-14 can be seen to be in marked contrast to each other. In the first period, the decreasing stream of new investment came after the collapse of a rush of land investment. In the later period, the decrease in new investment was brought about by the more stringent financial conditions which predated the fall in land prices and the final collapse of the boom conditions in western Canadian agriculture. Thus, throughout the period, the stock of British direct investment in the financial sector of the Canadian economy was related to agricultural development. The preponderance of British investment in the loan and mortgage businesses ensured this close link.

DISTRIBUTION

There were never more than eight British direct investments in the distributive sector of the Canadian economy during the period under review. From about 1900 to 1911, the stock of this investment was almost static. Even with the formation of a few firms in 1899 and 1900 and later in 1911, the extent of investment was small. Few firms were established as agents for parent British manufacturers. Most manufacturers in Great Britain appear to have carried on their agency business by contract to Canadian firms or, occasionally, to British companies. A rare exception was the P.J. Mitchell Company Limited, classified here as a general distributive company, which acted as an engineering agency for nine major machine tool and equipment manufacturers in Great Britain. However, there was no corporate link between it and the British manufacturers. The company was established in 1911 by a British engineer and undertook contract engineering work. Much of this work was the specification of equipment which the company then supplied in its agency capacity.[60]

58 'Canadian Bank of Commerce, Review of Business Conditions, 1912,' *The Economist*, 1 Feb. 1913, 221

59 *The Economist*, 3 May 1913, 1213

60 The Canadian P.J. Mitchell Company Limited, *P.R.O.*, 116323/BT/3120075. By 1913 the company had successfully completed contracts with the Dominion Iron and Steel Company of Nova Scotia and the Canadian Pacific Railway.

TABLE 3.15
Business activities of some British direct investments in the Canadian utilities and service sector, 1890–1914

Type of business (main activity)	Number of firms
(1)	(2)
Hydro-electricity and allied services	4
Shipping and port facilities	4
Hotels and apartments	3
Railway and canal construction-contractors	3
Home construction	2
Telephone and telegraph service	2
Publishing/entertainment	2

Most of the distributive British direct investments in Canada were small firms. Their activities were seldom national in scope. Few, as will be seen later, ever became profitable.

UTILITIES AND SERVICE

The stock of British direct investment in the utilities sector remained relatively stable over the period 1906–14. This was unlike the pattern of investment in all other sectors of the Canadian economy. Firms in this sector were spread over a wide range of economic activities and thus were less subject to economic fluctuations associated with one industry's output. Some of the larger companies engaged in several business activities. For instance, the British Columbia Transport Company Limited was formed in 1912 to operate a steamboat transport business. Within a year the company was supplying water power at New Westminster, as well as owning gravel and granite property. The company then used these assets as security for a debenture issue of nearly $250,000 which financed the purchase of a Canadian company, the Pitt Lake Brick and Cement Company Limited, from the Westminster Properties Limited.[61]

Although the pattern of British direct investment in Canadian utilities and services was diffused over a wide range of activities (see Table 3.15), it was concentrated geographically. Never less than 90 per cent

61 British Columbia Transport Company Limited, *P.R.O.*, 122735/BT/31/20749

of this investment during the period 1890–1914 was located in the province of British Columbia. Unlike most British companies in Canada, virtually all the major firms in this sector (capitalized at over $485,000) acquired existing Canadian firms as a basis for their new businesses.

MANUFACTURING

The manufacturing activities of British direct investments were to a large extent concentrated in the food and beverage industry and within that area they were active only in brewing, sugar refining, and the salmon fisheries. Here the investments in brewing all pre-dated 1900 and by 1914 only two firms were operating. The founding of two breweries in 1891 and 1895, the registration of the Acadia Sugar Refining Company Limited in 1893, and the opening of two salmon canning firms contributed to the growing stock of British direct investment in manufacturing during these early years. Except in the salmon fisheries, this increased investment was the result of the takeover of failing domestic firms by British entrepreneurs. The output of the fishing industry was relatively unaffected by the depressed conditions of the early 1890s and this increasing stock of investment was not inconsistent with the general lack of economic growth in manufacturing during this early period.[62] For most of the period 1890–1914, there were more British companies in the food and beverages industry than in any other single area of Canadian manufacturing. This, however, was not reflected in the proportions of the stock of investment within manufacturing since the salmon canning companies tended to be very small (see Table 3.16 and Appendix B).

The salmon fishing industry in British Columbia grew from a value of output of $3.5 million in 1890 to $13.8 million in 1913.[63] In 1905, the fisheries in British Columbia became larger than those in any other province of Canada (by current value of output) and remained so for the entire period. In real terms the growth in canned salmon output grew from 419,211 cases (1 case = 48 1-lb tins) in 1889 to 1,247,212 cases in 1901 and 1,400,252 cases in 1913.[64] British direct investment had established itself early in the history of this industry

62 'Annual Reports of the Department of Marine and Fisheries, 1896,' *Sessional Papers*, No. 11A (Ottawa, 1897), xiv

63 'Annual Report of the Department of Marine and Fisheries, 1913–1914,' *Sessional Papers*, No. 39 (Ottawa, 1914), xliii-xliiv

64 See above, various years.

TABLE 3.16
Number of British direct investments active in the Canadian manufacturing sector, selected years, 1890–1914

Years	B.C. fisheries	Other food and beverages	Other manufacturing	Total
(1)	(2)	(3)	(4)	(5)
1890	2	1	1	4
1894	2	3	1	6
1898	2	4	5	14
1904	5	4	5	14
1909	5	3	7	15
1914	6	3	12	21

and by 1892 was producing, in real terms, about 35 per cent of the canned salmon output. By 1895 there were 40 companies operating in this industry. Of these businesses all but two were domestic Canadian firms. However, the two British firms accounted for about 15 of the 49 canneries being operated on the Pacific Coast of Canada. These British owned canneries still produced about 30 per cent of the industry's output. British direct investment in the West Coast fisheries maintained their large percentage of industry output throughout the period 1890–1914. Growth in the participation of domestic Canadian businesses was matched by new British investment, and by 1914 there were six active British firms in this industry, with most of them operating more canneries than the average domestic firm.[65]

Not all the British investments in the Pacific fisheries were in the salmon canning business. One notable exception was Canada Fish Products Limited, which produced a light oil and fertilizer from fish offal. In 1913/14 the company produced 97.6 thousand gallons of oil and 589 tons of fertilizer from its factories on the Fraser River and Howe Sound.[66] As a direct participant in both the salmon canning industry and its by-products, British direct investment throughout the period 1890–1914 remained an important source of capital for the British Columbia fisheries.

The British direct investments that were active in the other sections of the Canadian manufacturing sector were widely distributed among different types of economic activity. Tweed and flannel, mica

65 'Report of Marine and Fisheries,' 1914, intro., 257
66 The Canada Fish Products Limited, *P.R.O.*, 87805/BT/31/17691

boiler coverings, organs and pianos, cement, agricultural machinery, tar and chemicals, and cigarettes were among the goods produced. Dominion Tar and Chemical Company Limited and Imperial Tobacco Company of Canada stood alone as large manufacturing concerns under direct British control in Canada. Because of their size these multi-plant companies were responsible for the large increases in the stock of British direct investment in Canadian manufacturing in the period immediately prior to World War I.

SUMMARY

During the 1896-1900 mining boom in Canada, British direct investment in mining was greater than that in the entire mining sector of Latin America. By 1911, British direct investment in Canadian land and real estate was greater than the comparable British investment in American land. (It was only the registration of one very large company in 1912 that raised the amount of investment in United States land (Col. (6), Table 3.17).[67] British investments in financial companies had also, by 1913, become greater in Canada than in the United States. Thus, between 1890 and 1914 in both rural and urban real estate and finance, British interests in North America had switched the majority of their operations from the United States to Canada. It might also be noted that Lewis, in her survey of British direct investments in the United States, found very few subsidiaries of British manufacturing firms operating branch plants. It appears that few British firms were undertaking this type of activity prior to 1914 in either Canada or the United States.

Although British direct investment overseas in this period was not solely restricted to the regions of recent settlement, there does appear to have been a heavier concentration in those areas.[68] Induced by the economic expansion in these developing regions, this investment provided further capital for development. Some direct investment was made in the infrastructure, but generally funds were attracted into projects and businesses that were considered to bear more risk.[69] In most regions mining attracted British capital. Agriculture and agricul-

67 Lewis, Appendix C, p. 574 and Rippy, p. 68

68 See, for example, the investments in Ceylonese tea and rubber companies in: N. Ramachandrin, *Foreign plantation investment in Ceylon, 1889-1958*, Ceylon, 1963.

69 Simon, 'Canada,' p. 249

TABLE 3.17
Some comparative estimates of British direct investment overseas, selected sectors and years* ($ 000's)

		Canada		U.S.A. (Lewis)		Latin America (Rippy)	
Sector	Year	No. of cos.		No. of cos.		No. of cos.	
(1)	(2)	(3)	(4)	(5)	(6)	(7)	(8)
Mining	1900	205	92,174	—	—	121	59,510
	1913	80	43,907	—	—	144	—
Land (and related companies)	1900	22	11,072	23	32,301	30	52,380
	1911	65	21,713	15	19,235	—	—
	1914	99	36,283	15	32,665	77	—
Banking	1913	1	4,850	—	—	—	89,793
Finance	1913	43	29,701	7	24,003	27	—
Manufacturing	1900	16	9,093	—	—	17	24,250
	1913	23	46,211	—	—	43	—
Aggregate	1900	278	142,745	—	—	—	—
	1913	286	191,512	—	—	—	—

*For 1890 comparisons see Table 2.5.

SOURCES: calculated from data presented in: Lewis, Appendix C, 573–4; Rippy, 36–65

tural finance also accounted for large amounts of direct investment.[70] Investment in primary industries and the provision of financial capital for further real capital formation through pastoral finance and land companies was of critical importance to regions which were 'capital-scarce' and which depended heavily for economic growth on the performance of the exports of primary products.

In each sector of the Canadian economy the pattern of investment varied. Investment in mines was so large by 1900 that despite its subsequent decline, it still remained the major area of British direct investment. Throughout the period after 1900 there was a lessening concentration of this investment in any one particular sector of the Canadian economy. This was largely due to the post-1909 increases in new investment. However, in the sectors other than mining, the stock of British direct investment did display variations that distinguished each area of business enterprise from any other. All, however, displayed similar trends and the resulting series of aggregate stock of direct investment reached a peak for the entire period in 1914. Aggregate British direct investment in Canada was not spread evenly throughout Canada, but tended to be concentrated in the western provinces. Rough checks indicate that the stock of British direct investment in Canada was a significant proportion of all British business enterprise overseas.

70 See, for example, N.G. Bultin, *Investment in Australian economic development, 1861-1900*, Cambridge, 1964

4

'Compelled to suspend'

Although the stock of British direct investment in Canada increased throughout the period 1890-1914, it neither increased as rapidly as its American counterpart nor as quickly as the gross flow of direct investment would suggest. This was a consequence of the liquidation (voluntary and compulsory) of British companies and occasionally a result of companies phasing out their Canadian business activity. Individual business failures rest, for the most part, on the unprofitability of the business ventures. Later in this chapter, the record of individual profitability is examined and some generalizations are made which explain the poor performance of British enterprise in Canada. First, however, it is necessary to isolate the immediate or proximate causes for the withdrawal of British direct investment in Canada.[1]

CAUSES OF BUSINESS FAILURE

Of the British companies that had participated in the premature land boom in western Canada in the late 1880s ten were liquidated between 1890 and 1896. Most of these companies were liquidated

1 The failure rate of British direct investments in Canada was considerably higher than the failure rate of all Canadian commercial concerns during the period 1900-14. In any year the former was never less than 7.29 per cent while the latter was never more than 1.44 per cent. Even the non-mining British companies displayed a higher failure rate than domestic firms. During the collapsing phase of the Yukon-British Columbia mining boom, disinvestment as a proportion of the level of paid-up capital remained high. After 1904 and up to the eve of World War I this rate declined to an average 5.33 per cent for the period. However, this was still substantially above the Canadian average. Bradstreet's figures reprinted in *The Canada Yearbook* (Ottawa, 1918), pp. 543-5

voluntarily when it became evident that the shareholders would not receive the short-term profits that had originally been expected. The limited evidence suggests that these firms sold off the bulk of their assets in Canadian rural and urban land to other business enterprises and to private individuals who wished to hold the land on a longer term speculation.[2] As in the case of the Vancouver City Land Company Limited, liquidation at least provided the shareholders with some return.[3]

The immediate causes for the liquidation of British direct investments in Canadian mining were generally of three types. First, companies often ran short of working capital, could not meet their current expenditures, and were forced to suspend operations. Second, mining companies which floated fixed-interest securities often had to be liquidated because they could not meet the interest payments. Third, mining companies often chose to liquidate when their mines were depleted and had no market value rather than acquire new ones by reinvestment. Although these features were more pronounced during the period of the mining boom, they appear to have been the main determinants of the failure of British mining companies from 1890 to 1914.[4]

During the mining boom many companies ran into immediate difficulties as a result of inadequate provision for working capital. Current receipts from the sale of mineral output seldom matched expectations and these firms quickly found themselves either unable to carry on normal operations or facing the demands of creditors for the payment of current debts. Voluntary or compulsory liquidation usually followed. For example, Hardie Cinnibar Mines Limited, founded in 1901, was forced to suspend operations in 1903 when it was faced with a lack of working capital. The company then drifted into a period of permanent inactivity, and was liquidated by being struck-off the list of registered companies.

Occasionally, British mining companies exacerbated the problem of a shortage of working capital by the excessive use of fixed-interest debt to provide both working capital and the funds for capital expenditures. Even before the fall in phosphate prices in 1893 the Gen-

2 Sweet Water Ranche and Supply Company of Leeds England Limited, *P.R.O.*, 25269/BT/31/3978; Canadian Pacific Colonization Corporation Limited, *P.R.O.*, 25997/BT/31/4066

3 The Vancouver City Land Company Limited, *P.R.O.*, 29272/BT/31/4484

4 It is not possible to quantify the number of mining firms liquidated for each of these reasons.

eral Phosphate Corporation Limited, which operated in the Province of Quebec, was forced by the debenture holders to surrender control of the company to debenture trustees. (The company had floated a $1,000,000 issue of first mortgage debentures in 1890.) Finally, after repeatedly failing to meet the interest payments, the debenture holders failed to pass the company's accounts in January 1893. The Court liquidator noted: 'The failure of the company was attributed to insufficiency of working capital and to the fall in the phosphate market. It would appear that the failure is also due to the manner in which the company was financed in 1891 ...'[5]

Many of the British mining companies in Canada suddenly found themselves with relatively worthless assets in mines that failed to produce the quality of ore expected of them. In addition, only some of the larger non-ferrous metal and coal mining companies followed a policy of reinvestment. The others, and most of the smaller firms in the mining sector, did not make any use of depletion accounts in order to reinvest and spread risk over several producing mines. Of course, many of the British mining companies, especially in the gold mining section of the sector, were formed only to exploit one particular mine, capture quick profits, and then liquidate. The companies were liquidated as soon as the mine was depleted and had no market value. In April 1910, the following letter was received by the Registrar of Joint-Stock Companies in London:

> Dear Sir,
>
> I beg to acknowledge the receipt of your circular letter of the 6th. inst. asking for a return of the Alice Broughton Mining Company Limited, No. 79637.
>
> Unfortunately, this company ceased operations and work was suspended at the Mine, situate in British Columbia, in the year 1905, since which efforts have been made to sell the Mine, but so far without success. When a sale is effected the Company will be wound up properly.[6]

Having distributed its cash balances between the seven shareholders, the company subsequently requested that it be struck off the register as it had 'no funds, no assets.'[7] Apparently the value of the assets (the mine) were worth less than the trouble of keeping the company registered.

5 *The Mining Manual*, 1894
6 The Alice Broughton Mining Company Limited, *P.R.O.*, 79637/BT/31/10540
7 See above.

British direct investments in Canadian land were similar to those in the mining sector in that neither type of company undertook vigorous reinvestment policies. Usually one tract of land was purchased, subdivided, and sold off. The initial assets were never replaced and the company remained in business until its holdings of land were totally sold off. During the period 1905–1914, when twelve British land companies were liquidated, the business failures were precipitated by a lack of current receipts either to meet fixed-interest debt charges (to fund some development of the property) or to meet the balance of payments on the purchase price of the property. The subsidiary of the Canadian Agency Limited, the Southern Alberta Land Company Limited, failed when it could not pay the interest charges on its bonded debt. (As mentioned earlier, this debt had been used to finance a large irrigation scheme.) On the other hand, the Edmonton-Strathcona Land Syndicate Limited was liquidated by Court Order in mid-1914 when it could not keep up the payments on the property mortgage held by the London branch of the Canadian Bank of Commerce.[8]

After the fall in land prices in 1913, British land companies were faced with the alternative of selling their land holdings at a loss or holding them until prices rose again. Most chose to remain in business. However, World War I, the cessation of active management from Great Britain, and the problems associated with furnishing the companies in Canada with funds to meet expenses, such as taxes, caused many firms to liquidate or to become inactive (and later to be struck off the register). The Newcastle Canadian Investment Company Limited 'was compelled to suspend operations shortly after 1914, and what funds it had were used in paying Taxes in West Vancouver until two years ago, (1927) when the Company found itself unable to continue further payment of Taxes. In consequence, all of its assets have been sold by the Municipality of West Vancouver to defray Taxes now overdue.'[9] This company's experience was typical of many of the British direct investments in Canadian land although few continued to pay taxes for so long a period.[10]

8 The Edmonton-Strathcona Land Syndicate Limited, *P.R.O.*, 100324/BT/31/18612.

9 Newcastle Canadian Investment Company Limited, *P.R.O.*, 121734/BT/31/20637. My brackets

10 Kaleden Fruit Lands Development Company Limited, *P.R.O.*, 116425/BT/31/20087; Western Canada Grain Lands Unit Company Limited, *P.R.O.*, 116890/BR/31/20130

The British financial companies exhibited a greater capacity for survival than either British mining or land companies in Canada. No British direct investments in Canadian finance were liquidated during the decade of the 1890s. The only liquidation that can be attributed to the post-1890 change in the land market was the Bristol and West of England Canadian Land Mortgage and Investment Company Limited. This financial company stopped issuing dividends to common shareholders in 1893 and effectively ceased business in 1897. However, it was not until 1906 that the debenture holders forced the company to wind-up its affairs. Similarly, although not connected with the prairie land market, the British Columbia Corporation Limited was forced by its bond holders in 1907 to liquidate. In contrast, however, the liquidation of the Canada Settlers' Loan and Trust Company Limited was voluntary so that the company's accumulated cash balances might be distributed to its shareholders. This company was one of the few British finance companies with an apparently limited time horizon.

There were only ten liquidations between 1910 and 1914, most of the larger British direct investments in the financial sector survived. In part they survived because they were more flexible in adjusting their asset portfolios. Furthermore they did not have limited time horizons and were accordingly more apt to undertake new investments in Canada. However, the post-1914 balance sheets of some of these companies reveal that, after mid-1913, they often tended to retreat from mortgage extension in Canada and gradually repatriated their assets. More companies bought securities in Great Britain as a substitute for Canadian mortgages.[11] It was this characteristic that gave them a fairly good survival record after 1914.

In this section attention has been paid to the immediate causes of the British business failures in Canadian mining, land, and finance. The liquidations of the British mining companies were often precipitated by a shortage of working capital, an inability to service their fixed-interest debt, and the depletion of their mines. The British direct investments in land shared some of these symptoms. In both areas there was an implicit realization, in the formation of some companies, that these investments were not intended to be long-lived. The failure of British financial companies was sometimes attributed

11 This was especially true of the Scottish companies: Caledonian and Dominion Investment Company Limited, *S.C.R.O.*, 8092 Diss.; The British Canadian Trust Limited, *S.C.R.O.*, 7466; The British and American Mortgage Company Limited, *P.R.O.*, 11382/BT/31/14568.

to the burden of bonded debt payments that could not be met, but for the most part these companies avoided a high mortality rate by policies of reinvestment.

The financial structures of the British direct investments also betray a source of corporate weakness, the excessive dependence on the British capital market for equities and fixed-interest securities. This was most striking in the case of financial companies.

Canadian loan companies and building societies relied heavily on deposits, debentures, and other fixed-interest debt, as well as on equity liabilities. Only one of the British direct investments in the financial sector was empowered by the Canadian government to accept deposits from the Canadian public, the Trust and Loan Company of Canada. Most British direct investments in the Canadian financial sector relied only on the sale of equities and fixed-interest debt to finance increases in assets. Over the period 1893–1906 the modest expansion of the property loan assets of the Canadian companies was financed by an increase in bonded debt (much of which was issued on the British market).[12] On the other hand, the British companies during this period did not expand their assets by this or any other method. As a result, for the entire period 1890–1913 there was, on average, a lag of about two years between the adjustment of British companies to a position similar to that of most Canadian companies. The correlation coefficients between the stock of paid-up capital of British companies and the level of total liabilities, the level of investment in property loans, and the level of investment in property of the Canadian companies were highest when there was a lag of two years. (The coefficients were +0.82, +0.84, and +0.81 respectively.) During the boom years of 1909 to 1913 the British financial companies expanded their paid-up capital liabilities (and assets) at a much faster pace than the Canadian companies expanded their total liabilities. (The average annual rate of growth was 33.1 and 14.1 per cent respectively.) By the boom period, therefore, the British companies did not lag behind the domestic companies in the provision of loans and land mortgages.

Investments by British companies in both land and finance were linked through the response to the wheat boom, the increased land prices, and the necessity of financing these increased land prices

12 Many Canadian financial concerns maintained close contacts with the British capital market. These contacts were not always with London as some Canadian trust companies issued their bonds, etc., through Edinburgh. See the *Stock Exchange Year-Book*, various issues.

TABLE 4.1
Assets and liabilities of all Canadian loan companies and building societies, selected years, 1890–1914

		% Assets		% Liabilities			
Years	Total asset and total liabilities ($ 000's)	Total loans	Prty. owned	Paid-up capital	Deposits	Debs. payable	Others
(1)	(2)	(3)	(4)	(5)	(6)	(7)	(8)
1890	122,887	89.9	10.1	31.1	14.6	43.5	11.8
1895	142,781	84.5	15.5	28.4	14.0	40.1	17.5
1900	152,640	80.9	19.1	32.0	13.1	33.6	21.3
1905	208,081	78.1	21.9	25.1	10.7	31.2	33.0
1910	347,548	67.0	23.0	16.9	7.4	26.8	48.9
1913	478,658	63.5	14.5	14.5	6.8	22.2	56.5

SOURCE: 'Annual Report of the Department of Trade and Commerce,' *Sessional Papers*, no. 10 (Ottawa, 1915), Part IV, 42

through mortgages and loans. That there was no corporate link between these various types of British investments is underlined by the fact that 20 of the 57 financial companies were registered in Scotland, whereas in the land sector there were only 10 Scottish companies out of a total of 123 registered as British. The similarity in the patterns of British direct investment in the Canadian land and financial sectors was a result of investment in western expansion. In particular the expansion of British land investment was contingent on the expansion of the entire Canadian financial sector, of which the British financial companies were a part. These patterns of investment were not directly associated with the land sales of the single, largest corporate holder of land in Canada, the Hudson's Bay Company, despite the fact that it was a British company.[13] The extensive reliance on the British capital market to the exclusion of Canadian savings effectively impeded the ability of the British financial companies to respond to profitable investment opportunities in Canada. Domestic companies, as evident in Table 4.1, were in marked contrast. In other sectors, where British firms relied more heavily on equity securities as a method of finance, this was no less true.

13 Of course, this is not to argue that these land sales were either not important or were not indirectly important to the extent of British business activity.

ACQUISITIONS

There was no widespread movement on the part of Canadians or Americans to acquire British businesses in Canada. Nevertheless, there were examples of several of the potentially profitable British direct investments succumbing to take-overs during the period 1890–1914.[14] For instance, after the failure of land sales to materialize in the early 1890s the Canadian shareholders of the Canada North West Land Company Limited[15] managed to achieve effective control of the company. In 1893 the assets of the firm were officially registered in Canada when a new Canadian company was formed, with the same name, and the original company liquidated.

The Asbestos and Asbestic Company Limited also passed to different ownership as non-British shareholders began to exercise more control. This company, which had been formed in 1897, acquired from American owners an asbestos mine and mill in Quebec. The purchase in 1897 allowed Americans, because the sale was partly in vendors shares, to sit on the board of the company; they reasserted control in 1901 when the British firm failed to secure enough capital for the re-equipment of the mine and mill at Danville, Quebec. 'In 1901 the control of the majority of the shares was obtained by Mr. Cannon, one of the directors, who has found the necessary funds for the re-equipment of the mine, and for floating indebtedness, etc., and a large new mill with all the latest machinery has been constructed. The management at the same time was transferred to New York.'[16]

The structure of Canadian banking was radically changed by a merger movement in the early years of this century. The total number of banks in Canada was reduced from 36 in 1900 to 22 in 1914, and to 10 in 1928 almost entirely by the process of large concerns amalgamating with smaller ones.[17] In the majority of cases the mergers were at the request of the smaller banks and occurred when a bank was 'rapidly approaching an insolvent condition or had reached the point where (perhaps through absence of aggressive management)

14 Discussion here is limited to the acquisition of British companies (assets and debts) by non-British interests. It does not include discussion of the cases where the assets *alone* were acquired by non-British concerns.

15 Macdonald, p. 244

16 *The Stock Exchange Year-Book, 1904*, 1494

17 B.H. Beckhart, 'Fewer and larger banks,' *Money and banking in Canada*, ed. E.P. Neufeld (Toronto, 1964), p. 197

it was unable to compete successfully with the larger institutions.'[18] One of the first banks to be absorbed by a large Canadian bank was the Bank of British Columbia which was taken over by the Canadian Bank of Commerce in 1900.[19]

Prior to 1914 only a few British direct investments were acquired by non-British interests in general. However, after 1914, and especially in the 1920s, the stock of British direct investment in Canada was greatly diminished by the take-overs of some major British companies. In 1918 the Bank of British North America fell prey to the merger mania among Canadian banks when one of its major rivals, the Bank of Montreal, took control. Within the first five years of the 1920s three of the largest of the British companies in Canada disappeared through take-overs by non-British interests. The British Columbia Electric Railway Company Limited was slowly acquired by Canadian shareholders and then transformed into a Canadian firm. The Mond Nickel Company Limited was acquired by its major competitor, the American International Nickel Company Limited. In 1920 an American direct investment in Canada, Imbrie and Company 'acquired the controlling interest in the Acadia Sugar Refining Co., Ltd., of Halifax, one of the oldest and best-known Canadian refineries, whose control had formerly been held in Scotland.'[20] Within these few years after World War I, the largest British firms in several sectors had been transferred from British to Canadian or American control.

The reasons behind the take-overs varied. Many of them were simple transfers of control from one group of shareholders to another. As in the cases of Acadia Sugar Refining and Mond, others were caused by the overt action of other firms which wished to add these profitable enterprises to their own companies. None of the major post-1914 take-overs could be foreseen in the period 1890–1914. However, these acquisitions and the resulting diminution of British direct investment aided in giving this form of British investment in Canada its temporary characteristics.

RETURNS TO SHAREHOLDERS

Only a very few of the British direct investments in Canada achieved dividend rates that compared favourably with those of domestic

18 See above.

19 As indicated later in this chapter, the bank was less profitable than its Canadian counterparts.

20 Lewis, p. 298

TABLE 4.2
Dividends from British direct investments as a percentage of the outstanding paid-up value of share capital, 1890–1914

	Sectors							
	Mining	Oil	Land	Timber	Finance	Utilities	Mfg.	Total
	(1)	(2)	(3)	(4)	(5)	(6)	(7)	(8)
1890	1.37	—	3.00	—	6.88	—	7.02	3.83
1891	1.46	—	1.97	—	7.02	—	4.74	3.30
1892	0.90	—	2.02	—	7.21	—	2.88	3.09
1893	1.25	2.38	3.91	—	6.50	—	0.18	3.55
1894	2.20	2.38	3.00	—	5.04	—	1.01	3.15
1895	1.35	2.38	3.34	—	4.05	—	2.88	2.96
1896	0.61	—	3.38	—	3.79	—	1.82	2.06
1897	0.56	—	3.28	—	4.21	—	0.26	1.44
1898	0.56	0.31	3.58	—	3.07	—	1.44	1.12
1899	0.74	0.37	3.75	1.17	4.43	0.77	1.69	1.41
1900	1.29	0.37	4.27	—	4.51	0.69	1.92	1.71
1901	0.96	0.47	3.99	—	4.59	0.69	2.83	1.60
1902	0.45	0.36	6.74	—	4.68	0.74	2.60	1.61
1903	0.97	0.83	7.66	—	5.34	0.49	2.77	1.98
1904	0.45	1.02	10.73	—	5.54	0.92	2.36	2.05
1905	0.42	1.31	13.95	—	5.73	1.10	1.84	2.35
1906	1.01	0.94	15.89	—	6.56	1.49	4.43	3.71
1907	0.81	0.46	20.65	—	6.61	1.69	2.81	4.26
1908	1.16	0.27	14.28	—	6.53	2.36	1.22	3.51
1909	1.23	—	17.26	—	7.17	2.41	1.21	4.06
1910	1.31	—	21.16	—	5.03	2.91	1.43	4.89
1911	1.34	—	21.32	—	4.01	4.09	1.67	5.42
1912	2.09	—	9.93	—	4.40	3.69	1.49	3.79
1913	1.37	—	3.55	—	5.19	3.63	5.39	3.63
1914	1.93	—	4.02	—	3.48	2.32	3.90	2.97

Canadian firms. Indeed, many shareholders could have secured higher returns, with comparable risk, simply by purchasing the shares of Canadian equities issued in Britain, such as those of London and Canadian Loan and Agency Company Limited of Toronto, which like many Canadian financial companies, issued equities through Edinburgh. Selected issues of Canadian equity securities were usually available on the London Stock Exchange.[21] As evident in Table 4.2,

Name	1890/94	1895/99	1900/04	1905/09	1910/14
(1)	(2)	(3)	(4)	(5)	(6)
The Right of Way Mines, Ltd.	n.a	n.a	n.a	24.5	2.5
War Eagle Consolidated Mining and Development Co. Ltd.	n.a	5.4	0.6	3.1	3.2
Nipissing Mines Co. Ltd.	n.a	n.a	n.a	19.4	29.0
The Canada Landed and National Investment Co. Ltd.	6.75	6.0	6.0	7.0	8.25
Canadian Northern Prairie Lands Co. Ltd.	n.a	n.a	n.a	10.0	11.3
Bank of Ottawa	8.0	8.6	9.0	10.0	10.8
London and Canadian Loan and Agency Ltd.	8.0	6.8	6.0	6.0	6.8
Ontario Loan and Debenture Co.	7.0	6.5	6.0	6.6	8.2
Montreal Street Railway Co. Ltd.	8.0	9.2	10.0	10.0	10.0
Bell Telephone Company of Canada, Ltd.	8.0	8.0	8.0	8.0	8.0
Consumers' Gas Company of Toronto, Ltd.	10.0	10.0	10.0	10.0	10.0
City Dairy Company Ltd.	n.a	n.a	—	0.5	3.8
The Canadian Salt Company Ltd.	8.0	8.0	8.0	8.0	8.0
British Columbia Fishing and Packing Co. Ltd.	n.a	n.a	n.a	n.a	7.0
The Dominion Cotton Mills Company Ltd.	6.0	6.0	2.5	5.0	5.8

SOURCE: *The Canadian Annual Financial Review*, Toronto; various issues *The Stock Exchange Year-Book*, various issues

21 *The Average Dividend Rate on Common Shares of a Sample of Quoted Canadian Companies (%)*

the search for relatively greater returns was not rewarded. The question then becomes how many of these British investments yielded positive returns to their shareholders. Despite the substantial body of literature on the pre-1914 overseas business activities of British firms few attempts have been made to examine their profitability.[22] Simple measures often present a misleading impression of the returns to the shareholders because of the failure to adjust for the time structure of dividends and capital losses. The latter is critical when most of the businesses exploit natural resource staples or are linked to staple production. Results of the British experience in Canada are presented in Table 4.3.

Since the criteria for any investment project must be that the estimated net present value (NPV) should be greater than zero, the evidence presented here shows that the entrepreneurs met with varying success in estimating the NPV's of the direct investments in Canada. Where there are hazards in investing that do not lie within the control of the investor the NPV is premised by some probability distribution of risk. For example, in mining there is the risk that within a given field or geological area a discovery of mineral deposits will not be made. Thus, the risk will be determined by a variety of factors that include the state of technical knowledge in mining geology and exploration and the endowment of the resource field. (This risk could be randomly distributed where the state of technical knowledge is low.)

The investor in the mining and allied resource industries is then faced with two problems. First, he must evaluate the risk associated with any mining activity or exploration. Second, he must attempt to estimate the NPV of the investment project. The actual NPV, as calculated here, is calculated only in retrospect after adjustments have been made for the size of the discovery, the quality of ore, the movement in raw material prices, and the other factors that the entrepreneur cannot foresee.[23] The entrepreneur's estimate may then vary

22 See Rippy, J.F., Jackson, W.T., Ramachandran, N., and Stone, I., 'British long-term investment in Latin America, 1856-1913,' *Business History Review*, 42, No. 3 (1968), 311-39; C.C. Spence, *British investment and the mining frontier*, Ithaca, N.Y., 1958; and S.H. Frankel, *Investment and return to equity capital in the South African gold mining industry, 1887-1965*, Oxford, 1967.

23 C. Morse, 'Potentials and hazards of direct international investment in raw materials,' *Natural resources and international development*, ed. M. Clawson (Baltimore, 1964), p. 370

TABLE 4.3
Rank of profitable new British direct investments in Canada, by IRR, 1890-1914

Name	Dates	Assumptions made	Principal activity	IRR (%)	NPV ($000's)
Mining					
North-West Mining Co. Limited	1897-1900	C	Silver/lead	190.2	139
Mond Nickel Co. Ltd.	1900-1914[a]	—	Copper/nickel	14.0	5,151
Western Canada Investment Co. Ltd.	1907-active	—	Coal/coal leases	11.4	329
Cobalt Town Site Silver Mining Co. of Canada Ltd.	1906-1914	—	Silver/lead	4.5	132
British America Corporation Ltd.	1897-1914	—	Silver/lead	2.5	—
Tyee Copper Company Limited	1900-1922	—	Copper/silver	2.5	—
Canadian Mining Corporation Ltd.	1914-1917	—	Silver	2.3	—
Casey Cobalt Mining Co. Ltd.	1907-1920	B	Silver	1.6	—
Nimrod Syndicate Ltd.	1899-1905[b]	—	Gold	1.6	—
Land					
Dominion and British Lands Co. Ltd.	1910-1912	C	Land	155.6	305
Canadian Resources Development Ltd.	1911-1935	—	Land	33.2	786
Canadian City and Town Properties Ltd.	1910-1925[d]	—	Urban land	22.4	603
The Calgary and Edmonton Co. Ltd.	1902-1927	—	Land	19.4	1,487
Canadian Land and Ranche Co. Ltd.	1895-1926	B	Land/agric.	14.6	234
Kamloops Land and Development Co. Ltd.	1911-1939	B	Land	10.3	5
British Columbia Farms Ltd.	1911-1920	B	Land/agric.	7.9	12
Manchester Canadian Investment Ltd.	1912-1925	B	Land	5.8	7
The Coldstream Estate Co. Ltd.	1906-1922	—	Land/agric.	5.7	82
The Nelson (B.C.) Syndicate Ltd.[c]	1899-1929	B	Land	4.8	36
Canadian Real Properties Ltd.	1902-1909	C	Land	4.7	22
Qu'Appelle, Long Lake, and Saskatchewan Land Co. Ltd.	1891-1902	—	Land	3.3	30
Alberta Land Co. Ltd.	1906-1951	B	Land	3.0	4
Bowness Estates Ltd.	1912-1924	B	Urban land	2.5	—
Canadian Finance and Land Co. Ltd.	1912-1924	B	Land	2.5	—

TABLE 4.3 (continued)

Name	Dates	Assump-tions made	Principal activity	IRR (%)	NPV ($000's)
Land (continued)					
Port Arthur (Current River) Estates Ltd.	1911-1915	B	Urban land	2.3	—
Western Canadian City and Town Lands Ltd.	1912-1934	—	Urban land	0.9	—
Western Canada Townlots Ltd.	1912-1929	B	Urban land	0.5	—
Western Canada Land Co. Ltd.	1906-1954	—	Land	0.2	—
Finance					
Dominion Agency Ltd.	1911-1913	C	General finance	305.9	34
Anglo-Canadian Finance Co.	1906-1922	—	General finance	20.6	137
Yorkshire Trust Limited	1890-active	—	General finance	9.9	32
Northern & Dominion Mortgage Co. Ltd.	1913-1920[d]	—	Mortgage loans	9.5	43
Edinburgh North American Investment Co. Ltd.	1892-1917	—	Mortgage loans	6.4	49
Canada North Western Investment Co. Ltd.	1912-1930	B	General finance	5.3	3
Caledonian Canadian Investment Co. Ltd.	1911-1921	B	General finance	4.4	6
British Canadian & General Investment Co. Ltd.	1911-1925[d]	B	General finance	3.1	—
Scottish Canadian Mortgage Co. Ltd.	1912-?	B	Mortgage loans	3.0	—
Caledonia & British Columbia Mortgage Co. Ltd.	1912-1927	B	Mortgage loans	2.3	—
Western Canada Trust Ltd.	1906-1928	—	Mortgage loans	2.2	—
Dominion of Canada Investment and Debenture Co. Ltd.	1910-active	—	General finance	2.1	—
Scottish & Canadian General Investments Co. Ltd.	1910-active	—	General finance	2.0	—
Canadian Merchants and General Trust Ltd.	1911-1949	B	Mortgage loans	1.3	—
Investment Corporation of Canada Ltd.	1911-active	—	General finance	0.6	—
Edinburgh Canadian Mortgage Co. Ltd.	1912-?	—	Mortgage loans	0.1	—
Timber					
Canadian Pacific Timber Co. Ltd.	1906-1908	C	Timber	328.0	757
Canadian Pacific Sulphite Pulp Co. Ltd.	1906-1910	C	Pulp mill	33.7	876

TABLE 4.3 (continued)

Name	Dates	Assumptions made	Principal activity	IRR (%)	NPV ($000's)
Distribution					
Cariboo Trading Co. Ltd.	1900-1933	B	General trading	0.9	—
The Maple Creek (Canada) Cattle Co. Ltd.	1897-1916	C	Cattle trading	0.8	—
Utilities					
British Columbia Transport Co. Ltd.	1912-1917	B	Water/general	22.0	130
Dominion Building Co. Ltd.	1913-1926	B	General construction	9.9	2
Compagnie Générale du Port de Chicoutimi	1906-1942	B	Port facilities	4.6	10
British Columbia Telephones Ltd.	1898-1905	C	Telephone	4.1	38
British Columbia Electric Railway Co. Ltd.	1897-1923	—	Power/tramway	2.4	0.0
Manufacturing					
Saint Mungo Canning Co. Ltd.	1899-1921	B	Salmon canning	10.4	23
Anglo-British Columbia Packing Co. Ltd.	1891-1926	B	Salmon canning	8.4	504
Acadia Sugar Refining Co. Ltd.	1893-1926	—	Sugar refining	3.1	124
Dominion Tar and Chem. Co. Ltd.	1903-1929	B	Tar/chemicals	2.9	5
The following lists the yield on the 1890 market value of the shares of companies active in the period 1890-1914 but founded prior to 1890					
General Mining Assoc. Ltd.	1825-1900	—	Coal mining	12.8	
Vancouver City Land Co. Ltd.	1888-1912	C	Urban land	128.2	
The Canada North-West Land Co. Ltd.	1882-1893	CA	Land	8.77	
Canadian Pacific Land and Mortgage Co. Ltd.	1888-1896	A	Land	7.36	
Scottish Ontario and Manitoba Land Co. Ltd.	1879-active	—	Land	6.82	
British Columbia Land and Investment Agency Ltd.	1887-1925[d]	AB	Land	6.61	
Manitoba and North West Land Co. Ltd.	1889-active	AB	Land	5.68	
Hudson's Bay Company	1670-active	—	Land	5.03	
Land Corporation of Canada Ltd.	1881-1926	—	Land	4.45	

TABLE 4.3 (continued)

Name	Dates	Assumptions made	Principal activity	IRR (%)	NPV ($000's)
1890 market value of shares of companies active in 1890-1914 but founded prior to 1890 (continued)					
New Oxley (Canada) Ranche Co. Ltd.	1886-1904	A	Agric.	0.98	
The Canada Company	1826-1953	—	Land	0.40	
North of Scotland Canadian Mortgage Co. Ltd.	1875-active[c]	—	Mortgage loans	11.65	
Trust and Loan Company of Canada	1845-active	—	Trust & loan	11.45	
Bank of British North America	1840-1918	—	Banking	4.10	
Bank of British Columbia	1862-1900	—	Banking	3.29	
Canada Settlers' Loan and Trust Co. Ltd.	1889-1910	—	Mortgage loans	3.32	
North British Canadian Investment Co. Ltd.	1876-1932	—	General finance	1.77	

[a]The calculation was made up to the 1914 reconstruction.
[b]This represents the active life in Canada.
[c]The last documented asset in Canada was in the late 1920s.
[d]Approximate date of last known assets in Canada

NOTE: The above table documents the long-run internal rates of return (IRR) on the initial cost to the shareholders of acquiring the equity stock. All share acquisitions were accounted for. These calculations are based on the net present value (NPV) formulation

$$NPV = -C + R_1 / (1+i) + R_2 / (1+i)^2 + \dots R_n / (1+i)^n + S / (1+i)^n,$$

where C is the cost of acquiring shares, $R_1 \dots R_n$ the stream of returns, S the market value of the equities on liquidation or in 1914, and i the interest rate. The equation is set to zero and solved for the unknown rate of return r which is substituted for i. Assuming the alternative return to be the yield on British consul bonds, the NPV has been given, where positive, to indicate the scale of the investment project. When information could not be obtained it was necessary to invoke assumptions which might give a reasonable approximation of the IRR. These are

A = par value is assumed for the shares in 1890,
B = par value is assumed for the shares in 1914,
C = par value is assumed for the replacement of shares by those in a new company.

If there is a bias it is one which would make the businesses seem more profitable than they, in fact, were. Consequently all companies not listed here made capital losses. Companies founded prior to 1890 defy the computation of an IRR. However, appended to this table are the yields generated on the 1890 market value of their equities.

widely from the actual *ex post* calculation. The ability to estimate closely the actual NPV will be determined by the experience the entrepreneur has had in assessing the patterns of development in the industry and by his technical expertise. Thus, there are two elements to be considered by the investor. When, as in the case of British direct investment in Canada, the problems of estimating the risk factor and the returns are complicated by problems of distance and communications.

The calculations show for the mining sector that the majority of British entrepreneurs were unsuccessful in, at least, equating the NPVs of their projects to zero. However, was this inability to invest profitably in Canadian mining determined by (i) the chance of discovering minerals or by (ii) the miscalculation of how to (or indeed whether to) bring these resources into production in order to yield a positive return?

The Canadian experience prior to 1914 suggests that British investors attempted to avoid the impact of the riskiness associated with mining exploration and development. By buying existing mineral claims and developed properties or mines an attempt was made to minimize this risk. Original prospecting and early development of mineral claims was carried out not only by Canadians but by American direct investors. The British companies refrained.[24] Few British companies engaged in exploration. 'British engineers are not prospecting.'[25] Rather, the British companies bought the mineral rights from vendors. The Yuneman Gold Fields Limited, when registered in 1902, was empowered to acquire mines, lands, and mining rights but seemingly was not empowered to explore for minerals.[26] It finally bought eight mining claims from a British Columbia promoter.[27] This tendency was as evident in coal as it was in gold mining. The majority of British companies bought their mineral claims from Canadian or American companies or individuals. Even where it appears that a British company had bought its rights from its own 'development agency' – or a British promoter – the names of the specific mining claims often betray the original developer and prove that the British agency was the intermediary.[28] A mining paper noted: 'Many of the

24 *The British Columbia Mining Record*, August, 1896, 24

25 *The Canadian Mining Journal*, 1 Sept. 1913, 556

26 Memorandum of Association, The Yuneman Gold Fields Limited, *P.R.O.*, 73087/BT/31/16788

27 See above.

28 Similar name patterns can be found for mineral claims in the western United States and British Columbia; see Spence. The names of the mineral claims

registered companies have done nothing more than merely register their articles of incorporation. The promoters, Micawber-like, are awaiting for something to turn up. In other words, they are looking for someone to buy them out.'[29]

There is probably no simple explanation why British firms seemed to prefer to invest in developed mining claims. Part of the reason must be the intense activity of the Canadian and American development mining companies. In late 1895, the British Columbia government recorded the registration of 52 domestic, 35 American, and 2 British mining companies.[30] It was not until 1896 that British companies were formed in any number to invest in British Columbia. Small companies with virtually no physical capital could be created and register claims before any British entrepreneurs were aware of the new mining area. Part of the explanation can also be sought in the growing conservatism of the London market for mining capital. The period 1890–1914 witnessed the eclipse of the single entrepreneur and the concentration of more mining company formation in the hands of the large financial houses. These houses preferred developed properties where the 'present value' could be calculated more easily.[31]

If, as is claimed, the risk of undeveloped properties was avoided, the full explanation must be sought in the ability to estimate the actual NPV of the resource claim acquired. First, there were those firms which intended to invest solely for speculative purposes. Companies bought, at inflated prices, mineral claims on which a capital gain could be made by resale at even higher prices. The almost traditional losses followed.

For the British companies formed to mine mineral claims actively the record of estimating the actual NPV was no better. Turrentine-Jackson claims that in the western American mining areas, in the 1890s, 'the English worked systematically, employing the services of the best equipped experts in the world to conduct painstaking investigations.'[32] This, if true, contradicts the characteristics of the British

were registered by the first owner and after that were invariant to ownership. Mining companies often adopted the name of the mining claim in their title. Thus, the Idaho-Alamo Consolidated Mines Limited (which bought the properties from the Scottish Colonial Gold Fields Limited) was registered as a Scottish company and took its name from the Idaho and Alamo mining claims.

29 *The British Columbia Mining Record*, Nov. 1896, 12

30 See above, Jan. 1896, 27

31 *The Financial Times*, cited in the *Canadian Mining Journal*, Sept. 1913, 556-7

32 Jackson, p. 198

companies in the Canadian mining areas. Almost unanimously the Canadian mining press berated the British investments for employing inexperienced mining engineers and inexperienced mine managers.[33] Often the survey conducted for the British firm was done by a mining engineer out from the Rand or Rhodesia to analyse the unfamiliar complex ore deposits of British Columbia.[34] A familiarity with local mining conditions was a prerequisite for the formation of a profitable mining venture. While noting the re-opening of the 'Old Bruce Mines' in Ontario, a press editorial specifically approved of the combination of 'English capital and an American mining engineer.'[35]

Poor technical expertise in new fields of mining, such as the non-ferrous metal discoveries, and in areas where the ores were found in complex forms, appears to be the main reason for the inability of British companies to estimate profitability satisfactorily. Often profitable opportunities were overlooked as in the instance of a mining site which was evaluated as worthless by a British engineer but which subsequently proved to be the basis of a profitable operation. In this case it was claimed that the engineer did not spend enough time on the site.[36] The poor record of profitability illustrates the optimistic technical evaluations which led many of the British mining companies to overevaluate the NPV of the mineral claims. It was the inability to gauge the NPVs of mining claims that led British companies to accept risks that were not compensated for in Canadian mining. By paying prices for mining claims at inflated levels, the British companies invariably ensured that they could not achieve a NPV greater than zero. It was not without a slight sense of wonder that *The Economist*, in 1890, noted of all British mining investments overseas: 'Why then ... if mining ventures are as a whole so eminently unprofitable, are they so constantly being brought out successfully, here, as well as upon various provincial stock exchanges.'[37]

33 *The British Columbia Mining Record*, June 1896, 12; *The Canadian Mining and Mechanical Review*, Oct. 1901, 223

34 *The British Columbia Mining Record*, August 1896, 24

35 *The Canadian Mining and Mechanical Review*, Feb. 1901, 21. The preference of British mining companies overseas for British mining engineers may have been a reaction to some unfortunate experiences with domestic engineers in Australia and the United States. The engineers were often the sole source of information for the investors.

36 *The British Columbia Mining Record*, May 1899, 17. Other cases are cited in mining journals.

37 *The Economist*, 22 Feb. 1890, 236

Similarly, in the Ontario oil fields, where average annual output per well was falling through the 1890-1914 period, the British oil companies usually lacked local knowledge. As in the mining industry, large British oil companies tended to acquire property with producing wells rather than explore for new well sites. Although these oil wells were reported on by qualified engineers, the engineers seldom had much experience in Canada. The engineer who reported for the East Tilbury (Canada) Oilfields Limited, Sir B. Redwood, was no less than the official adviser on petroleum matters to the Admiralty, the Home Office, the India Office, the Port of London Authority, and the Corporation of London. Yet, despite his optimistic reports on the quantity of reserves, the company successfully produced oil for only the three years from 1909 to 1911.[38] The reliance on this type of poor technical advice accounts almost exclusively for the stark unprofitability of British direct investment in the oil and petroleum sector.[39] Notably, although not profitable by the standards used here, the Ontario Lands and Oil Company Limited with its local manager and local field manager was one of the longest lived British oil investments in Canada.[40]

Profitability in the land sector, with the exception of the few purely agricultural firms, was totally dependent on land prices and the ability to predict them. This applied equally to rural farmland and urban real estate. The ability to predict land prices was not a simple process. It was first necessary for the entrepreneur to gauge the appropriateness of the price asked by the vendor. Then it was necessary to judge the future of land prices in conjunction with certain views on the course of rural - mostly in the west - and urban development during the periods of expansion. A judgment had to be made by the entrepreneur about the length of time it would take land prices to reach a level where company sales could begin. Next, the entrepreneur had to ensure that the firm had a sound enough financial structure to withstand the contingencies which would arise

38 *Business men at home and abroad*, 1912-13, ed. H.H. Bassett (London, 1912), p. 339

39 'Extract from the Annual Report of the Maritime Oilfields Limited, March, 1914,' *The Oil and Petroleum Manual* (London, 1914), 94. 'The most unsatisfactory feature of the development during the year has, however, been the somewhat marked decrease in the pressure of gas at the wells, this indication pointing to the fact that the life of the wells may be shorter than the Directors from the reports of the exports anticipated.'

40 *The Canadian Oil Book*, 1929 (Montreal, 1929), 83

if errors had been made in prediction. Some influence over the land price was exercised by those companies undertaking improvements, but this, in turn, often caused a financial strain on the companies.[41] It appears from the timing of the registrations of subsequently profitable companies, which coincide with the rise in Canadian land prices in the 1880s and from 1906 to 1913 that prediction was easier and the margin for error larger in an ebullient market.[42] Since both urban and rural Canadian land prices were widely quoted in the British press, there can be little validity to the claim that unprofitable investments were a result of imperfect knowledge. Rather, profitability was a matter of the entrepreneurs anticipating price rises without being carried away by the optimism created by the booms.

The financial sector, by providing funds for purchases by individuals, helped determine expenditure on land. Profitability in the financial sector was often claimed to be only a function of the good management of loans and mortgages portfolios.[43] It is, nevertheless, true that during the years from about 1898 to 1903 domestic funds were slightly cheaper than British funds and narrowing profit margins in the loan and mortgage business combined to reduce the chances of profitable British direct investment in financial activities. Notably, no profitable British investments were initiated in this field from 1894 to 1905.[44] The majority of profitable British financial investments were formed in the boom of the pre-1913 years, when the demand for mortgages was increasing most rapidly.

Significantly, financial companies did not behave like the land companies. Land companies were similar to the mining firms which were in the business of depleting fixed resources. Among the profitable financial companies there was a tendency to diversify their portfolios. This was especially marked after the 1913 slump in real estate prices. An examination of the post-1914 balance sheets of these financial companies showed that many of them had, over time, divested

41 A.G. Bradley, *Canada in the twentieth century* (London, 1905), pp. 365-6; *The Stock Exchange Year Book, 1915*, 827; and *The Economist*, 3 Oct. 1914, 198

42 Since many land companies bought blocks of land for the purpose of resale to other land companies, the timing of the purchase of land often determined whether the land had passed through the hands of intermediaries or not.

43 A.D. Besant, 'Report of the paper read to the Canadian Institute of Actuaries, Canada,' *The Economist*, 26 Dec. 1914, 1099

44 W.T. Easterbrook, *Farm credit in Canada* (Toronto, 1938), pp. 43-9

themselves not only of their mortgage loan holdings but also, later, of their entire Canadian assets.[45]

Both the British owned banks in Canada formed prior to 1890 had dividend yields that were slightly lower than most Canadian banks in the period 1890-1914. They earned 6 and 7½ per cent respectively for the decade prior to 1900. This compared to an 8 per cent average yield for the Imperial Bank of Canada and a 10 per cent average yield for the Bank of Montreal, two of the country's leading domestic banks.[46] The Bank of British Columbia in 1900 and the Bank of British North America in 1917 were both absorbed into large Canadian banks. This entire period was noted for a vigorous merger movement in Canadian banking when many of the less profitable banks were eliminated.[47]

In the distributive, utilities, and manufacturing sectors there were no general characteristics that explain profitability. Nor were there any apparent general characteristics that explain unprofitability. However, nearly all the British direct investments were of unincorporated branch status in Canada. Company policy, for the most part, remained the perogative solely of the British head office. (This was least true of the financial and land sectors, where the authority to grant mortgage loans or sell individual farm units had to be delegated.) Even after World War I, a Canadian government department was to comment on the fact that British direct investments tended to be of the early form of corporate status, the unincorporated branch.[48] Certainly, the United States direct investors after 1900 were increasingly using the new form of corporate organization, the subsidiary firm.[49] By this method a certain amount of company policy and decision-making authority was transferred to the host country. (Of course, this transfer of authority may have been a function of United States law rather than an actual willingness to decentralize the decision-making power.)

Decision-making authority far removed from the area of economic activity was bound to slow down the process of reaching economic decisions. It was also likely to lead to less well-formed decisions, be-

45 For example, Canada North Western Investment Company Limited, *S.C.R.O.* 8203, Diss.; North of Scotland Canadian Mortgage Co. Ltd. *S.C.R.O.*, 642

46 R.M. Breckenridge, *The Canadian Banking System, 1817-1890* (New York, 1895), pp. 464--9

47 Backhart, pp. 196-205

48 *Canada as a Field for British Branch Industries*, 5

49 Lewis, pp. 294-6

cause of the unfamiliarity with local Canadian conditions. When this failure to delegate responsibility was coupled with the unwillingness to engage local expert opinion, the results usually led to unprofitability.[50]

In the aggregate, profits were made only in the land and financial sectors of the Canadian economy.[51] Even these modest profits were more than offset by the substantial collective losses registered in the other sectors. In Canadian mining alone British investors lost over $150 million between 1890 and 1914. British entrepreneurship in Canada did not produce many profitable companies. The reluctance to invest in manufacturing and the inability to adapt to the Canadian conditions of extensive resource development produced this unfavourable profitability record.[52]

50 A visitor to Canada in the early 1900s noted: 'I have been often asked in Canada whether English companies operating there were promoted for the purpose of providing berths for the incompetent person in England - the incompetency of course, in some cases being merely a lack of experience, which, however, is just as bad for the owners and shareholders.' (Bradley, p. 339)

51 Calculated as the sum of the NPVs for all firms founded between 1890 and 1914

52 The same unwillingness to adapt has been claimed to exist domestically. D. Aldcroft, 'The entrepreneur and the British economy, 1870-1914,' reprinted in the *British economy 1870-1917*, eds. D. Aldcroft and H. Richardson (London, 1969), pp. 141-67

5

Conclusions

For the most part British business enterprise in Canada achieved a poor profitability record during the two and a half decades prior to World War I. Consequently, British direct investments were liquidated more often than domestic businesses. Despite these general tendencies, many British controlled businesses were successful.

In the salmon canning industry, for instance, British ownership and managerial talent did combine to produce profitable companies (and many near profitable companies). The volatile nature of salmon catching and canning of course required that company policy be delegated to British Columbia. The British (most often Scottish) managers in British Columbia usually had long experience in this industry. The manager of the British Columbia Canning Company Limited, M. Johnston, had lived in the province for twenty-eight years, while H. Bell Irving of the Anglo-British Columbia Packing Company Limited was also a long-time resident of British Columbia.[1] There are similar examples of efficiently managed British firms in other sectors. Significantly, but beyond the scope of this study, the British Columbia Electric Railway, the Mond Company, and Acadia Sugar Refining all fell prey to take-overs from non-British interests in the post-war years. In none of these cases was any corporate weakness clearly visible.[2]

Earlier it was argued that a complete reliance on the British capital market was a source of financial weakness for many British direct in-

1 'British Columbia Fishery Commission Report, 1892,' Department of Marine and Fisheries, *Sessional Papers* (Ottawa, 1893), 328–52

2 P.E. Roy, 'Direct management from abroad: the formative years of the British Columbia electric railway,' *Business History Review*, 47, no. 2 (1973), 239–59

TABLE 5.1
Acquisition of existing Canadian businesses by British direct investments in the utilities and manufacturing sectors*

Direct investment	Canadian business or company acquired	Date
(1)	(2)	(3)
1 Anglo-Canadian Hotels Limited	King George Hotel Limited	1911
2 British Columbia Electric Railway Co. Ltd.	New Westminster and Vancouver Tramways Ltd.	1897
3 British Columbia Telephones Ltd.	Victoria and Esquimalt Telephone Co. Ltd.	1898
4 British Columbia Transport Ltd.	Steamboat business	1912
	Pitt Lake Brick and Cement Co. Ltd.	1913
5 Halifax Graving Dock Co. Ltd.	Chebucto Marine Railway Co. Ltd.	1885
6 Kettle River Power Co. Ltd.	Cascade Water, Power, and Light Co. Ltd.	1900
7 Port of Chicoutimi Co. Ltd.	La Compagnie Géneral du Port de Chicoutimi	1906
8 Acadia Sugar Refining Co. Ltd.	Halifax Sugar Refinery Ltd.	1893
	Nova Scotia Sugar Refinery Ltd.	
	Moncton Sugar Refinery Ltd.	
9 Bell Organ and Piano Co. Ltd.	Messrs. Bell and Co.	1890
10 Dominion Carpets Co. Ltd.	Dominion Brussels Carpet Co. Ltd.	1900

*Excludes the direct investments in breweries and salmon canning. All of the former acquired existing Canadian breweries. Many salmon canning investments acquired canneries both from other British investments and from domestic (Canadian) companies.

vestments. In the utilities and service sector, as well as in manufacturing, this was not the case. Ready access to the British capital provided new firms with the resources to take over a Canadian business. All but one major British direct investment (a paid-up capital greater than $485,000) in the utilities and service sector took over domestic companies as a prelude to conducting business in Canada (Table 5.1). The exception was the Marconi Wireless Telegraph Company of Canada Limited, which operated a trans-Atlantic cable service. These were not take-overs in the contemporary sense of one existing company acquiring another. In all the cases examined (including the investment in breweries) a new British firm was formed solely to take over an existing Canadian company. Included were a few companies in the manufacturing sector. In one instance the business had been owned by a Quebec company, and a special act of the Canadian Parliament was required before British interests could acquire it in 1906 ('An Act to Incorporate La Compagnié Générale du Port de Chicoutimi, 4 Edward VII c. 86').[3]

In the utilities sector, 72.2 per cent of the equity issues of $25,340 thousand of British investments during the period 1890–1914 were made by those companies that had acquired Canadian firms. In the manufacturing sector, take-overs, with only two exceptions, were limited to the food and beverage industry. Although there is very little evidence to tell us which side initiated the take-over proceedings, most appear to have taken place for the same reason, a shortage of business or working capital. Some of the Canadian firms, such as the breweries and a hotel company, required fresh injections of capital to avoid liquidation. The forming of British direct investments to take over these firms was designed to facilitate access to the British capital market. In the process amalgamations were also undertaken. The Acadia Sugar Refining Company Limited and the Halifax Breweries Limited both amalgamated several small Canadian businesses. The former acquired three sugar refining firms, and the latter combined four breweries in Nova Scotia and Prince Edward Island.[4] Other take-overs appear to have been designed in order to secure capital for expansion. This can only be observed after the fact, but is confirmed by the subsequent expansion of companies like the British Columbia Electric Railway Company Limited,[5] British Columbia

3 Port of Chicoutimi Company Limited, *C.R.O.*, 87434 Diss.

4 Acadia Sugar Refining Company Limited, *S.C.R.O.*, 2522, Diss.

5 G.W. Hilton and J.F. Due, *The electric interurban railways in America* (Stanford, 1960), p. 422

Transport Company Limited, and the Bell Organ and Piano Company Limited.

British direct investment in the Canadian utilities sector and in some parts of the manufacturing sector was largely a response to individual profit opportunities rather than general investment in a sector where profits could be made. The advantage that these investments commanded was their access to the British capital market. As a result of this tendency to acquire Canadian businesses and because the economic advantage of the British firms did not dictate a specific type of investment, British direct investment was diffused over a wide range of activities in these sectors.[6]

In 1912, H.P. Evans, the president of the Canada Provident Investment Corporation, commenting on the flow of British business capital to Canada, wrote: 'This flow of new money found its way into every Province and into almost every form of investment and the continuance of the remarkable industrial and agricultural development of the country must in part have been assured by this fertilizing stream of new capital.'[7]

Although new British direct investment in Canada during the period 1890-1914 was, in the short-run, almost solely determined by specific demands for capital in sectors of the Canadian economy, certain business conditions in Great Britain helped to facilitate this flow. These supply factors included rising share prices and an increased willingness on the part of entrepreneurs to undertake business activities of all types through the registration of new nominal capital. However, when business activity in Great Britain is measured by the peaks and troughs of the 'business cycle' (or changes in home investment), it is observed that the Canadian and British business cycles were not in phase. This was not a factor limiting new British direct investment in Canada. Rather, the negative, short-run relationship between British home investment and new British investment in Canada (of all types) was a consequence of the pull exerted by the demand for capital in Canada.

6 The utilities sector was concentrated geographically. This, unlike other geographic concentrations, might be explained in part by the fact that Canadian firms approached British investors. British firms in turn were most likely to favour areas such as British Columbia where there already existed a large stock of other British investment. Ease of communications, familiarity, and associated factors would encourage it.

7 *Handbook of the Canada Provident Investment Corporation* (for private circulation, London, 1912), p. 20

New British direct investment in Canada and British home investment moved inversely to each other over the course of the long swing. Over the entire period 1890–1914 this 'push' factor was a critical determinant of how much of the British public's savings was directed into new direct investment in Canada. However, the relationship between new British direct investment and domestic investment in Canada was a positive one. When British home investment was low, new British direct investment tended to be high because of the greater amount of British savings available for overseas investment and because investment in Canada had an attractive quality. New British direct investment in Canada, therefore, was determined by the complex forces that generated inverse long swings in British and Canadian investment.

Over the period 1890–1914 new British direct investment was a more variable process than new British portfolio investment in Canada. This was a result of the inherent character of direct investment which, because of its exclusive business nature, tended to be a riskier form of international activity. Business activity was not only riskier in that returns were not guaranteed but also in that the course of this investment in Canada was often directed into individual sectors which were likely to perform, from the point of view of profitability, in a manner not typical of a wider selection of businesses in the Canadian economy. Furthermore, the returns from direct investment dividends tended to vary more than they did from portfolio investment. The dividend payments of the British companies in Canada were co-cyclical with the Canadian business cycle and put proportionately less pressure on the Canadian balance of payments.

The quantitative evidence of this study confirms that British direct investment in Canada was present in significant amounts during the period 1890–1914. Nevertheless, this corporate activity must be judged a failure since British business enterprise did not persist as a major force in the Canadian economy. 'Failure' has been used here to define aggregate business performance. It has many dimensions, some of which at the level of individual firms do not imply irrationality or inefficiency on the part of British enterprise. Such was the case in the first major dimension of this failure.

The absence of any substantial direct investment in manufacturing is a striking feature of British business behaviour in Canada during the period under study. In this important respect it differed significantly from the American business penetration of Canada. Manufacturing firms had longer time horizons than many of the investments exploiting natural resources at this time and thus were better prepared to reinvest out of retained earnings. In turn, this helps to explain the persistence of American direct investment and the ephemeral quality of the British business presence. The vital question, however, still remains: why did the forces that attracted American branch plants not attract British branch plants. Stringent patent regulations, the high Canadian tariff adopted as part of the National Policy in 1879, tax inducements, as well as transportation cost barriers all acted as stimuli to the establishment of American branch plants.[8] The same forces, to a greater or lesser extent, were felt by British manufacturing firms which exported to Canada. The speedier response to these initial attractive forces on the part of the American firms was undoubtedly due to the proximity of the two countries and relatively longer duration of the depression of 1873 in Great Britain. Nevertheless, it is sufficient to note that the American response was to jump the tariff wall in order to expand their markets in Canada and that as a consequence the British market share must have declined.[9] If foreign manufacturing direct investment occurs as a response to tariff barriers and as a reaction to declining market shares,[10] it is still to be expected that British manufacturers would have established plants which, from the point of view of Canada, would produce import-substitute goods.

Import-substituting investments are those which tend to reduce domestic imports (or the exports of the donor country in which the manufacturer is initially located). Such foreign direct investment usually takes place after the company in question has achieved a high volume of export sales in a foreign market. This market becomes the host area when an assembly or production plant is built.[11] The impetus to switch from exporting to production in the host country may be, as noted, dictated by a tariff barrier or a desire to increase or defend a market share. In the host country imports are diminished by

8 Marshall, *Canadian-American industry*, 198–217; M. Wilkins, *The emergence of multinational enterprise* (Cambridge, Mass., 1970), pp. 135–48; and S. Scheinberg, 'Invitation to empire: "Tariffs and American economic expansion in Canada,"' *Business History Review*, 47, no. 2 (1973), 218–38

9 This is based on the assumption that the tariff levels of 1879 did qualify as an 'infant industry tariff.'

10 A.E. Scaperlanda and L.J. Mauer, 'The determinants of U.S. direct investment in the E.E.C.,' *American Economic Review*, 59, no. 4 (1969), 558–68

11 W.B. Reddaway et al., *Effects of U.K. direct investment overseas: an interim report*, University of Cambridge, Department of Applied Economics, Occasional Paper 12 (Cambridge, 1967), 33

the new investment which supplants the original manufacturing firm. The pre-condition of such international corporate development is the establishment of marketing agencies and distribution facilities which ensure sales and later provide the basis for expansion into production activities.

One of the classic examples of this type of corporate expansion is that of the British glass manufacturing company, Pilkington Brothers. In 1890 the company established warehouses and sales agencies in Montreal to expedite its sales in Canada. To cope with increasing Canadian sales, which grew from a value of $250,000 in 1890 to over $1 million in 1906, depots were opened in Toronto, Vancouver, Winnipeg, and Calgary.[12] Progress to a Canadian branch plant followed in 1914 when Pilkington entered a patent sharing agreement with the American Window Glass Company. In order to protect its Canadian market share the patent had to be operated or the protection was lost. At a cost of $1.25 million the company built a factory at Thorold, Ontario, which employed the patented 'cylinder process' of manufacturing plate glass. The English plant's exports to Canada were affected immediately.[13] Although the model of foreign manufacturing business penetration is confirmed in the case of this company, few other British enterprises had matured to branch plant status by the beginning of World War I.

Before the turn of the century most British manufacturers exporting to Canada commissioned their exclusive marketing rights either to independent agents or Canadian companies and few physical facilities were established for holding inventories in Canada. Advertising, especially in the capital goods industries, often referred the potential Canadian purchaser to a British telegraph address. Such evidence suggests a lethargic sales effort and is consistent with the view that the British manufacturers were either unwilling to defend (or expand) their market shares in at least one foreign market. Yet such primitive marketing arrangements were not typical of those in the entire twenty-five years prior to 1914 and the subsequent changes demonstrate that the British firms were concerned with the further erosion of their Canadian market shares by domestic producers and American branch plants.[14]

12 T.C. Barker, *Pilkington Brothers and the glass industry* (London, 1960), 168–96
13 Barker, *Pilkington*, pp. 194–6, 212
14 Information on sales agencies was collected by a survey of the business records of British firms held by the Quebec Provincial Archives (*Q.P.A.*).

A growing proportion of British manufacturers after 1900 abandoned the traditional marketing arrangements in Canada and replaced these with direct corporate participation. '... we furnish the affidavit of Henri Bilbert Nobbs who is the Canadian and American manager for Holbrooks Limited [foodstuff manufacturer] on this continent. You will see that it is not the purpose of this company to manufacture at all but merely to have within the Province a centre for which this Company's goods may be sold.'[15]

Increasingly through the immediate pre-war years British manufacturers registered in Canada with their own corporate identity. (Only rarely, however, did British companies create a Canadian subsidiary company, such as Debenham's (Canada) Limited, to supervise its Canadian activities.)[16] Most active in establishing the new sales outlets were the foodstuff, textile, and metal products manufacturers.[17] Along with the new corporate presence, new emphasis was also given to regular promotions in Canadian newspapers and journals. The 1908 edition of a major Canadian business guide contained large advertisements for, *inter alia*, the following British manufacturers:

Wm. Atkins and Co. Ltd.	Tool Manufacturer
Crosse and Blackwell	Foodstuffs Manufacturer
J. Kenyon and Company	Machine Knives Manufacturer
Turner, Naylor and Co.	Engineering Tool Manufacturer
Tyzack and Company	Engine Manufacturer
J. Wright	Iron and Brass Foundry
G. Wostenholm and Sons	Cutlery Manufacturer[18]

Although these companies for the most part established their new sales facilities in Montreal, some did penetrate the hinterland. For instance, increasing attention was paid to the newer urban areas in the west such as Calgary and Vancouver.[19]

If British sales agencies were evolving throughout this period, as the evidence suggests, British entrepreneurship in the manufacturing industries cannot be judged a failure insofar as there was an awareness of market shares and an increased willingness to defend them.

15 Holbrooks Limited, *Q.P.A.*, 2477/11

16 Debenham's 'Canada' Limited, *Q.P.A.*, 769/05

17 For example, Bovril Limited, *Q.P.A.*, 1966/06; Bagley and Wright Manufacturing Company Limited, *Q.P.A.*, 2105/04; and The Eagle and Globe Steel Company Limited, *Q.P.A.*, 269/14

18 *Canada's Manufacturers, Business and Professional Record and Gazetteer*, Toronto, 1908

19 For example, Craig and Rose Company Limited, *S.C.R.O.*, 4650

Yet it still remains true that before 1914 the American manufacturing presence in Canada had evolved to the branch plant stage whereas the British had not. If this is regarded as a tardy response to the growth of American branch plants and domestic manufacturing enterprises, then causality must lie in the failure of late nineteenth- and early twentieth-century British entrepreneurs to perceive quickly the investment opportunities in a Canadian market. Recent evidence, however, indicates that in this period British manufacturing entrepreneurs were more efficient than previous inquiries had supposed.[20] This revisionism opens up an intriguing line of argument. If late nineteenth- and early twentieth-century British manufactured exports were labour-intensive, there was no special need for the construction of British branch plants in Canada. That is, the relative labour-intensity of British manufacturing when compared with that of other industrial countries at this time, plus the highly skilled nature of that labour input, ensured the production of 'high quality' manufactured goods for which there were no substitutes.[21] Consequently, it may be argued that the delay in establishing a British manufacturing presence in Canada was a rational response to market forces. Such an argument must remain an exciting conjecture until more specific business histories reveal the quantitative information, particularly about market shares, which would allow a test of this proposition.

World War I brought a sudden end to the registration of British manufacturing sales and distribution facilities in Canada. In the following years many of the existing agencies were closed as the changed structure of demand diverted British manufacturers from their Canadian export market. It is as interesting as futile to speculate how these sales agencies might have developed had there been no war. Certainly, any potential British direct investment in Canadian manufacturing was further arrested despite the apparent growing concern over Canadian market shares in the pre-war years.

The second major dimension of the failure of British business enterprise in Canada was the weaknesses associated with the form of

20 The two basic positions are best summarized in 'The entrepreneur and the British economy, 1870–1914,' in *The British economy 1870–1939*, eds. D. Aldcroft and H. Richardson (London, 1969), pp. 141–67 and D.N. McCloskey and L.G. Sandberg, 'From damnation to redemption: judgements on the late Victorian entrepreneur,' *Explorations in Economic History*, 9, no. 1 (1971), 89–108

21 C.K. Harley, 'Skilled labour and the choice of technique in Edwardian industry,' *Explorations in Economic History*, 9, no. 4 (1974), 391–414

investment as undertaken at this time. These have been mentioned in previous chapters, but are summarized here:

(a) During the twenty-five years covered in this study the institutional nature of the British firms that invested in Canada changed little. Only six of these British direct investments were subsidiary companies with separate Canadian incorporations. As late as 1938 a Canadian government report noted that 'a comparatively large proportion of British direct investments in Canada is in enterprises which have no separate Canadian incorporation.'[22] The American direct investments, on the other hand, rapidly adopted the use of the foreign subsidiary type of company organization after 1900 for all types of business activity.[23]

The reluctance on the part of British firms to adopt this new form of organization was noticeable in all sectors of the Canadian economy in which British companies were active. Even in the distributive sectors British manufacturers did not adopt the subsidiary organization in Canada for the purpose of marketing or distributing their exports. The insistence by British companies upon the use of British technical experts and managers plus the fact that few managers appeared to be free to act independently indicate that the lack of adoption of the new form of company organization arose from a general unwillingness to decentralize decision-making authority. This resulted in poor or ill-timed decisions. The failure of many British direct investments can be attributed to the fact that technical and business matters had constantly to be referred to the British head offices. It was precisely this failure to adapt which led British business to accept higher risks in Canada where they were confronted with rigorous domestic and American competition.

(b) Although the British business enterprises which engaged in the issuing of mortgage loans were successful during the period 1890–1914, their complete reliance on the British capital market was a source of weakness. This weakness became apparent in the post-1913 years when the British economy was no longer in the position to maintain large exports of capital. Access to foreign savings may provide the foreign direct investor with an initial advantage over domestic enterprises, but it is unlikely that this alone ensures permanence. Indeed, Canadian history amply demonstrates that the ability of foreigners to mobilize domestic savings is an important determi-

22 *British and foreign direct investments*, p. 27
23 Lewis, throughout

nant of longevity (or success measured by survival).[24] An international flow of savings, unless accompanied by an international flow of entrepreneurship (or technology) is not a sufficient condition for establishing a lasting business presence. The ability (entrepreneurship) to mobilize domestic savings was absent even in the nominally profitable case of British enterprise in Canada during the period 1890-1914.

(c) In the sectors of the Canadian economy not directly linked to natural resource exploitation no significant concentration in a specific business activity was undertaken by British companies. Such a lack of concentration resulted in a more reserved attitude by the various branches of the British capital market to equity and fixed interest security issue. Further, when this lack of concentration was coupled with the British preference for management from head offices in Great Britain, no body of specialized managers was created.

(d) The absence of vigorous reinvestment policies on the part of British direct investments was a significant dimension of its failure to survive. Very few firms in the natural resource exploiting sectors attempted to diversify the risk of holding only one major asset. This apparently was not so much a learning-induced experience from an unprofitable business venture but a conscious policy to exploit a single asset over a short period of time. Short time horizons were evident in both the instances of profitable and unprofitable British direct investments in Canada.

(e) Finally, the British preference for direct business participation in sectors of the Canadian economy exploiting natural resources or in sectors linked directly to them led to many corporate weaknesses which were exacerbated by some of the characteristics previously mentioned. First, there was an excessive reliance on equity securities to mobilize business capital in Great Britain. This in itself was a symptom of the 'boom-bust' nature of business enterprises and the sales of equities which typified much of the period. Second, when British firms issued fixed-interest securities, they were seldom used to finance the acquisition of assets. Rather the issue of these securities became an expedient to raise working capital. Inevitably this caused the liquidation of the business when the interest payments could not be met.

The primary objectives of this study have been to quantify British direct investment for the period 1890-1914 and to analyse the failure

24 *Report of the Task Force on the Structure of Canadian Industry*, Ottawa, 1968

of British business to persist as a major element of the Canadian economy. Although the temporary nature of this direct investment can be explained by historical examination, many questions remain unanswered. Nevertheless, the evidence is both consistent and plentiful. British direct investment was not, by virtue of its business characteristics, dynamic enough to match that of the United States. It was the twenty-five years prior to World War I that proved most critical in shaping the subsequent profile of foreign business activity in Canada.

Appendices

Appendix A
Estimates of new British direct investment
in the Canadian mining sector, 1890-1914 ($000's)

Year	New companies registered	Nominal capital	Paid-up capital	Cash subscriptions	Bond issues
(1)	(2)	(3)	(4)	(5)	(6)
1890	3	4,930.0	1,058.5	587.9	4,850.0
1891	1	34.0	1,329.9	20.0	—
1892	5	2,619.0	1,986.4	943.6	72.8
1893	1	1,455.0	1,333.8	485.0	—
1894	3	515.7	557.8	315.3	77.6
1895	12	3,392.6	3,011.6	2,392.6	—
1896	34	19,037.7	11,307.7	4,388.9	106.7
1897	75	46,843.6	26,547.4	12,246.6	131.0
1898	65	37,811.1	30,088.3	15,034.9	493.2
1899	47	22,067.7	16,490.2	5,374.1	613.0
1900	31	23,229.1	21,350.2	15,150.2	—
1901	6	4,690.3	3,363.0	2,159.3	302.6
1902	11	7,800.2	5,737.3	2,537.5	—
1903	6	6,911.3	6,491.5	4,406.0	1,549.6
1904	4	1,486.5	1,086.3	261.8	7.8
1905	4	3,656.9	1,899.2	1,700.3	14.6
1906	12	2,391.5	2,173.0	800.4	518.6
1907	9	2,233.4	2,483.8	2,052.1	741.1
1908	13	3,210.3	2,556.6	1,077.3	322.5
1909	10	3,730.1	3,143.0	2,269.1	—
1910	14	5,038.5	3,035.3	1,903.1	—
1911	15	14,748.4	10,485.9	8,096.6	123.7
1912	7	2,801.5	2,196.0	940.2	60.6
1913	12	14,014.1	12,463.7	6,232.2	—
1914	12	23,641.5	13,641.5	12,271.4	—

Estimates of new British direct investment in the Canadian oil sector, 1890–1914 ($000's)

Year	New companies registered	Nominal capital	Paid-up capital	Cash subscriptions	Bond issues
(1)	(2)	(3)	(4)	(5)	(6)
1890	0	—	—	—	—
1891	2	2,309.3	2,207.9	2,042.9	—
1892	0	—	—	—	—
1893	0	—	—	—	—
1894	0	—	—	—	—
1895	0	—	—	—	—
1896	0	—	—	—	—
1897	0	—	—	—	—
1898	1	485.0	-142.5	—	—
1899	2	1,479.3	984.5	378.3	—
1900	0	—	—	—	—
1901	0	—	—	—	—
1902	1	485.0	284.1	133.7	—
1903	1	48.5	20.6	8.5	—
1904	1	58.2	48.6	48.6	—
1905	0	—	—	—	—
1906	1	388.0	264.4	21.9	—
1907	0	—	—	—	4.4
1908	1	727.5	485.0	485.0	85.4
1909	2	1,552.0	1,005.2	447.5	—
1910	5	1,801.8	1,409.5	1,085.9	—
1911	4	472.1	220.0	220.0	—
1912	1	291.0	226.9	48.5	—
1913	1	97.0	72.8	24.3	—
1914	5	625.6	382.5	110.6	—

Estimates of new British direct investments in the Canadian land sector, 1890-1914 ($000's)

Year	New companies registered	Nominal capital*	Paid-up capital	Cash subscriptions	Bonds issues
(1)	(2)	(3)	(4)	(5)	(6)
1890	1	48.5	26.7	26.7	—
1891	4	1,273.1	1,075.1	1,075.1	—
1892	0	36.4	16.8	16.8	—
1893	0	-100.9	-100.9	—	—
1894	0	—	—	—	—
1895	1	-76.6	290.9	290.9	—
1896	1	194.5	194.5	194.5	1,004.9
1897	1	218.3	49.3	34.8	—
1898	0	7.3	5.3	5.3	—
1899	1	97.0	97.0	97.0	—
1900	1	-97.2	-104.0	—	106.2
1901	1	218.3	218.3	218.3	—
1902	2	262.6	308.7	187.7	1,241.1
1903	0	-436.5	-172.3	—	—
1904	0	-630.5	-596.6	—	291.0
1905	1	-111.3	-122.5	—	—
1906	4	7,515.4	4,698.5	776.0	145.5
1907	1	-29.1	-16.8	—	—
1908	3	533.5	256.3	46.4	48.5
1909	5	1,882.0	1,079.2	127.9	1,526.8
1910	8	5,220.9	1,791.3	217.8	2,546.3
1911	26	8,904.5	4,694.0	917.6	2,772.2
1912	27	12,589.4	9,381.5	1,693.5	2,927.5
1913	12	6,594.5	6,151.1	1,239.0	2,628.7
1914	1	92.2	21.1	3.0	27.4

*Negative signs arise from company reconstructions.

Estimates of new British direct investment in the Canadian timber sector, 1890–1914 ($000's)

Year	New companies registered	Nominal capital	Paid-up capital	Cash subscriptions	Bond issues
(1)	(2)	(3)	(4)	(5)	(6)
1890	—	—	—	—	—
1891	—	—	—	—	—
1892	—	—	—	—	—
1893	—	—	—	—	—
1894	—	—	—	—	—
1895	—	—	—	—	—
1896	—	—	—	—	—
1897	1	485.0	180.4	160.5	—
1898	1	315.3	278.8	36.3	—
1899	—	—	—	—	—
1900	1	48.5	10.9	10.9	—
1901	—	—	—	—	—
1902	—	—	—	—	—
1903	2	160.1	139.9	62.3	116.4
1904	—	—	—	—	—
1905	—	—	—	—	—
1906	2	567.5	457.3	265.4	201.8
1907	1	848.8	485.0	1.5	363.8
1908	—	—	—	—	—
1909	—	—	—	—	—
1910	1	1,500.0	1,500.0	—	1,455.0
1911	2	3,152.5	1,452.3	244.5	713.0
1912	1	97.0	66.0	66.0	—
1913	—	—	—	—	—
1914	—	—	—	—	—

Estimates of new British direct investment in the Canadian financial sector, 1890-1914 ($000's)

Year	New companies registered	Nominal capital	Paid-up capital	Cash subscriptions	Bond issues
(1)	(2)	(3)	(4)	(5)	(6)
1890	3	6,743.9	1,162.5	1,162.5	86.3
1891	1	1,455.0	663.8	663.8	103.1
1892	1	485.0	72.8	72.8	317.2
1893	—	—	—	—	—
1894	—	—	218.3	218.3	—
1895	—	—	—	—	—
1896	3	1,358.2	333.1	308.8	—
1897	—	—	—	—	—
1898	—	—	119.1	119.1	—
1899	—	-1,697.5	-263.1	—	—
1900	—	—	—	—	—
1901	—	—	—	—	—
1902	—	-1,515.1	-58.7	132.4	—
1903	—	—	132.4	132.4	—
1904	—	-189.4	-59.2	130.5	—
1905	—	—	-239.1	—	31.6
1906	3	2,708.1	1,152.1	563.4	85.6
1907	2	1,721.8	228.6	228.6	—
1908	1	2,478.4	298.3	298.3	-3,325.6
1909	1	291.0	319.6	319.6	197.4
1910	9	15,714.0	6,654.2	6,608.8	3,920.6
1911	12	18,987.8	9,791.3	7,206.5	1,914.3
1912	9	6,409.3	3,211.9	3,183.5	5,555.7
1913	4	1,426.1	820.3	820.0	146.5
1914	1	48.5	87.7	87.7	253.7

Estimates of new British direct investment
in the Canadian distributive sector, 1890–1914 ($000's)

Year	New companies registered	Nominal capital	Paid-up capital	Cash subscriptions	Bond issues
(1)	(2)	(3)	(4)	(5)	(6)
1890	—	—	—	—	—
1891	—	—	—	—	—
1892	—	—	—	—	—
1893	—	—	—	—	—
1894	—	—	—	—	—
1895	—	—	—	—	—
1896	—	—	—	—	—
1897	2	147.9	75.9	73.5	—
1898	—	—	—	—	—
1899	1	97.0	48.5	48.5	—
1900	1	203.7	159.1	3.9	79.5
1901	2	106.7	29.8	29.8	—
1902	—	—	—	—	3.2
1903	—	—	—	—	—
1904	—	—	—	—	—
1905	—	—	—	—	—
1906	—	43.7	43.7	43.7	—
1907	2	—	—	—	—
1908	—	—	—	—	—
1909	—	—	—	—	—
1910	1	24.3	7.1	2.2	—
1911	—	—	—	—	—
1912	2	999.1	128.5	97.8	21.3
1913	—	—	—	—	—
1914	—	—	—	—	—

Estimates of new British direct investment in the Canadian utilities and service sector, 1890–1914 ($000's)

Year	New companies registered	Nominal capital	Paid-up capital	Cash subscriptions	Bond issues
(1)	(2)	(3)	(4)	(5)	(6)
1890	—	—	—	—	—
1891	—	—	—	—	—
1892	—	—	—	—	—
1893	—	—	—	—	—
1894	—	—	—	—	—
1895	—	—	—	—	—
1896	—	—	—	—	—
1897	1	1,794.5	1,552.0	1,552.0	—
1898	3	485.0	363.8	363.8	145.5
1899	1	679.0	849.6	849.6	—
1900	2	2,037.0	1,455.0	1,455.0	—
1901	—	—	—	—	—
1902	1	485.0	301.3	301.3	—
1903	1	5,363.8	5,363.8	5,363.8	1,091.2
1904	1	48.5	26.0	19.9	—
1905	1	242.5	229.9	50.4	—
1906	1	2,514.8	2,423.4	2,423.4	4.8
1907	—	2,425.0	2,425.0	2,425.0	1,425.9
1908	—	1,455.0	1,455.0	1,455.0	2,376.5
1909	—	—	—	—	—
1910	—	3,880.0	3,880.0	3,880.0	2,580.2
1911	1	242.5	242.5	242.5	3,633.1
1912	1	3,395.0	3,238.4	2,982.8	3,482.3
1913	3	897.3	191.4	190.2	6,339.0
1914	3	921.5	609.2	519.5	60.6

Estimates of new British direct investment in the Canadian manufacturing sector, 1890-1914 ($000's)

Year	New companies registered	Nominal capital	Paid-up capital	Cash subscriptions	Bond issues
(1)	(2)	(3)	(4)	(5)	(6)
1890	1	727.5	717.8	717.8	—
1891	2	1,940.0	723.8	723.8	485.0
1892	—	—	—	—	—
1893	1	2,910.0	2,716.0	2,716.0	485.0
1894	—	—	—	—	—
1895	1	242.5	501.0	161.5	331.7
1896	1	121.3	98.9	38.3	—
1897	3	3,055.5	2,837.6	2,784.2	—
1898	—	—	—	—	—
1899	5	1,276.3	873.8	538.7	339.5
1900	2	485.0	345.3	122.2	—
1901	1	194.0	72.5	67.7	—
1902	—	—	—	—	300.8
1903	1	145.5	178.5	149.4	—
1904	—	—	—	—	241.2
1905	—	—	68.9	68.6	—
1906	2	44.1	29.7	29.3	—
1907	—	72.8	24.3	24.3	—
1908	1	11,000.0	9,386.8	—	5.8
1909	1	72.8	63.4	43.8	87.3
1910	4	979.7	848.8	746.9	485.0
1911	6	2,362.0	1,775.1	1,312.4	258.0
1912	2	28,379.2	29,693.9	8,022.8	—
1913	—	10.6	-77.0	—	264.3
1914	—	—	—	—	43.7

Appendix B

The distribution of the stock of British direct investment in Canadian mining by area and type, selected years, 1890-1914

	1890		1900		1910		1914	
Area	$000's	%	$000's	%	$000's	%	$000's	%
(1)	(2)	(3)	(4)	(5)	(6)	(7)	(8)	(9)
Nova Scotia	2,552	33.6	—	—	—	—	—	—
British Columbia	1,793	23.6	63,652	69.1	17,230	43.1	13,119	24.1
Ontario	1,496	19.7	12,298	13.3	9,414	23.5	26,471	48.6
Quebec	1,717	22.6	1,111	1.2	946	2.4	817	1.5
Manitoba	—	—	26	—	—	—	—	—
Saskatchewan	—	—	—	—	970	2.4	970	1.8
Alberta	—	—	—	—	3,300	8.2	3,513	6.4
Yukon	—	—	13,203	14.3	4,515	11.3	8,509	15.6
Canada, unassigned*	40	0.5	1,883	2.0	3,537	9.1	1,122	2.1
TOTALS	7,598	100.0	92,174	100.0	40,010	100.0	54,921	100.0
Type								
Metallic minerals (excl. Gold)	1,797	23.6	45,928	49.8	19,212	48.0	33,709	61.8
Gold	725	9.5	37,134	40.3	10,150	25.4	11,258	20.6
Non-metallic minerals	1,644	21.6	122	0.1	939	2.4	1,302	2.4
Fuels (Coal)	3,392	44.6	2,842	3.1	6,219	15.5	5,138	9.4
Other	40	0.5	6,148	6.7	3,490	8.7	3,113	5.7
TOTALS	7,598	100.0	92,174	100.0	40,010	100.0	54,921	100.0

*In this Appendix the designation 'Canada, unassigned' indicates the investment of companies which was not restricted to one province. 'Other' then notes that investment in single provinces not explicitly noted above.

The distribution of the stock of British direct investment
in the Canadian oil sector by area and type, selected years, 1890–1914

	1890		1900		1910		1914	
Area	$000's	%	$000's	%	$000's	%	$000's	%
(1)	(2)	(3)	(4)	(5)	(6)	(7)	(8)	(9)
Ontario	1,939	100.0	1,108	24.5	3,511	—	1,892	60.4
Quebec	—	—	3,402	75.4	347	—	347	11.2
Other	—	—	—	—	485	—	892	28.5
TOTALS	1,939	100.0	6,510	100.0	4,344	100.0	3,132	100.0
Type								
Drilling and refining	1,939	100.0	1,444	32.0	2,456	56.5	2,055	65.6
Above plus distribution	—	—	3,055	67.7	1,379	31.7	518	16.6
Natural gas	—	—	—	—	509	11.7	485	15.5
Other	—	—	11	0.2	—	—	74	2.3
TOTALS	1,939	100.0	4,510	100.0	4,344	100.0	3,132	100.0

The distribution of the stock of British direct investment
in the Canadian timber sector by area and type, selected years, 1890–1914

	1890		1900		1910		1914	
Area	$000's	%	$000's	%	$000's	%	$000's	%
(1)	(2)	(3)	(4)	(5)	(6)	(7)	(8)	(9)
British Columbia	—	—	—	—	1,996	83.6	3,515	96.8
Alberta	274	100.0	274	37.2	274	11.6	—	—
New Brunswick	—	—	180	24.2	121	5.1	121	3.3
Other	—	—	289	38.4	—	—	—	—
TOTALS	274	100.0	745	100.0	2,392	100.0	3,636	100.0
Type								
Timber	274	100.0	564	75.6	771	32.3	2,015	55.4
Pulp & paper	—	—	180	24.2	1,621	67.7	1,621	44.6
TOTALS	274	100.0	745	100.0	2,392	100.0	3,636	100.0

The distribution of the stock of British direct investment in the Canadian land sector by area and type, selected years, 1890–1914

Area	1890		1900		1910		1914	
	$000's	%	$000's	%	$000's	%	$000's	%
(1)	(2)	(3)	(4)	(5)	(6)	(7)	(8)	(9)
British Columbia	1,028	5.7	1,009	9.1	2,361	13.8	5,058	13.9
Alberta	451	2.5	169	1.5	5,317	31.1	10,580	29.1
Saskatchewan	635	3.6	990	9.0	250	1.4	380	1.0
Manitoba	1,339	7.5	1,243	11.2	1,106	6.5	1,471	4.1
Ontario	889	5.0	889	8.0	1,030	6.0	1,856	5.3
Canada, unassigned	12,808	71.7	6,742	60.9	5,987	35.0	16,610	45.8
Other	732	4.1	29	0.3	1,037	6.0	279	0.8
TOTALS	17,882	100.0	11,071	100.0	17,088	100.0	36,283	100.0
Type								
Rural land	14,311	80.0	9,412	85.0	9,187	53.8	23,307	64.2
Urban land	732	4.1	49	0.7	1,063	6.4	4,337	12.0
Miscellaneous land	2,006	11.2	1,216	11.0	2,898	17.0	3,406	9.4
Agriculture and land	459	2.6	97	0.9	2,522	14.8	3,109	8.6
Agriculture	373	2.1	268	2.4	1,388	8.1	2,093	5.8
TOTALS	17,882	100.0	11,071	100.0	17,088	100.0	36,283	100.0

The distribution of the stock of British direct investment in the Canadian financial sector by area and type, selected years, 1890–1914

Area	1890		1900		1910		1914	
	$000's	%	$000's	%	$000's	%	$000's	%
(1)	(2)	(3)	(4)	(5)	(6)	(7)	(8)	(9)
British Columbia	3,977	31.4	1,613	14.8	688	3.8	4,613	5.6
Alberta	—	—	—	—	44	0.3	2,580	8.7
Manitoba	965	7.6	1,476	13.5	1,781	10.4	1,962	6.6
Ontario and Quebec	—	—	—	—	—	—	50	0.2
Canada, unassigned*	7,724	61.0	7,796	71.6	14,540	85.3	20,365	68.8
TOTALS	12,666	100.0	10,886	100.0	17,034	100.0	29,582	100.0
Type								
Mortgage and loan	4,421	34.9	5,004	46.0	8,771	51.5	16,903	57.1
General investment	485	3.8	1,031	9.5	3,413	20.0	7,828	26.5
Banks	7,760	61.3	4,850	44.6	4,850	28.5	4,850	16.4
TOTALS	12,666	100.0	10,886	100.0	17,034	100.0	29,582	100.0

*The majority was located in western Canada but was not specific to any one province.

The distribution of the stock of British direct investment
in the Canadian distributive sector by area and type, selected years, 1890–1914

Area	1890 $000's	1890 %	1900 $000's	1900 %	1910 $000's	1910 %	1914 $000's	1914 %
(1)	(2)	(3)	(4)	(5)	(6)	(7)	(8)	(9)
British Columbia	—	—	208	14.1	190	66.1	183	45.2
Alberta	—	—	52	19.0	52	18.6	52	13.1
Canada, unassigned	—	—	24	8.6	45	15.3	173	42.9
TOTALS	—	—	284	100.0	287	100.0	408	100.0
Type								
Distribution of U.K. goods for parent	—	—	49	17.2	76	—	69	16.7
General distribution	—	—	235	82.8	211	—	339	83.3
TOTALS	—	—	284	100.0	287	100.0	408	100.0

The distribution of the stock of British direct investment in the Canadian utilities and service sector by area and type, selected years, 1890–1914

	1890		1900		1910		1914	
Area	$000's	%	$000's	%	$000's	%	$000's	%
(1)	(2)	(3)	(4)	(5)	(6)	(7)	(8)	(9)
British Columbia	—	—	12,562	90.1	21,558	92.1	24,797	90.7
Nova Scotia	716	96.2	716	5.2	716	3.1	716	2.7
Other	—	—	—	—	415	1.8	1,070	3.9
Canada, unassigned	34	3.8	665	4.8	691	2.9	723	2.7
TOTALS	750	100.0	13,943	100.0	23,381	100.0	27,307	100.0
Type								
Transport	716	96.2	3,262	23.1	13,804	59.1	16,714	61.3
Communications	—	—	364	2.6	—	—	—	—
Construction	—	—	243	1.7	545	2.3	611	2.2
Other	34	3.8	10,073	72.4	9,032	38.7	9,981	36.6
TOTALS	750	100.0	13,943	100.0	23,381	100.0	27,307	100.0

The distribution of the stock of British direct investment in the Canadian manufacturing sector by area and type, selected years, 1890–1914

	1890		1900		1910		1914	
Area	$000's	%	$000's	%	$000's	%	$000's	%
(1)	(2)	(3)	(4)	(5)	(6)	(7)	(8)	(9)
British Columbia	378	20.2	1,251	13.8	1,417	8.7	1,271	2.8
Ontario and Quebec	1,494	79.8	4,617	50.8	1,237	7.6	1,250	2.7
Maritime Provinces	—	—	3,225	35.5	3,565	22.0	3,333	7.3
Other	—	—	—	—	558	3.4	633	1.4
Canada, unassigned	—	—	—	—	9,460	58.2	39,332	86.0
TOTALS	1,871	100.0	9,093	100.0	16,236	100.0	45,819	100.0
Type								
Salmon fisheries	426	22.7	1,251	13.8	1,242	7.6	1,087	2.4
Other food and beverages	727	38.8	3,709	40.8	3,468	21.4	3,008	6.6
Other	718	38.6	4,132	45.5	11,526	71.0	41,724	91.0
TOTALS	1,871	100.0	9,093	100.0	16,236	100.0	45,819	100.0

Bibliography

PRIMARY SOURCES USED FOR THE SURVEY OF BRITISH COMPANIES UNDERTAKING DIRECT INVESTMENT IN CANADA

Lists of British companies registered in Canada compiled from surveys of provincial registration data.
List of British Companies, Quebec, 1969
List of British Companies, Manitoba, 1969
List of British Companies, Alberta, 1969
List of British Companies, Quebec, 1972
'Tabulated List of Companies Incorporated, Licensed and Registered in the Province of British Columbia, Made up to 31st October, 1912,' in *Sessional Papers of British Columbia, 1913*, I (Victoria, B.C., 1914), B1-B104

List of Companies as at September 30th, 1937, Department of the Secretary of State, Ottawa, 1937

Index of Companies Registered, 17th July, 1856 to 30th June, 1920, Public Record Office

Index of Companies on the Register on 30th June, 1930, Public Record Office

Index of Companies on the Register on 30th June, 1937, Public Record Office

All the files of defunct companies held at the Public Record Office (P.R.O.) are foot-noted by registration number, box number, and file number. Most of these files are in box BT/31. Box BT/34 holds the liquidators' files on companies compulsorily wound-up. All company records held at the Companies Registration Office (C.R.O.) are footnoted by registration number only. It has been indicated if the company is defunct by the addition of the word 'Dissolved' (Diss.). The company files of the Office of the Registrar of Companies, Scotland (S.C.R.O.) has been footnoted in a similar manner.

The Mining Manual, London (1887–1912), continued as *The Mining Manual and Mining Yearbook*, London (1913–1915)

The Oil, Petroleum and Bitumen Manual, London (1910) continued as *The Oil and Petroleum Manual*, London (1911–1915)

The Stock Exchange Year-Book, London (1886–1919)

In order to avoid endless repetition of similar footnotes the following style has been adopted. Where there are no footnotes, all references to mining companies are from *The Mining Manual* and all references to oil companies are from *The Oil Manual.* The other company information not specifically footnoted is taken from *The Stock Exchange Year-Book.*

The business directories and newspapers listed below were also used in compiling the survey.

OTHER BUSINESS DIRECTORIES AND YEAR-BOOKS

The A.B.C. Western Canada Mining Directory and Yearbook, 1919, Vancouver, 1919

Canada's Manufacturers, Business and Professional Record and Gazetteer, Toronto, 1908

Canadian Industrials and Miscellaneous Companies, London, 1912

The Canadian Oil Book, 1929, Montreal, 1929

The Canadian Trade Index, Canadian Manufacturers Association, Toronto, various years

Directory of Oil Companies and Investors' Guide to the Calgary Oilfields, ed. C.C. Coffey, Calgary, Alta., 1914

Dominion Business Directory, Toronto, various years

Handbook of the Canada Provident Investment Corporation (for private circulation), London, 1912

Register of Defunct and Other Companies Removed from the Stock Exchange Year-Book, 1968, ed. W.S. Wareham, London, 1968

The Stock Exchange Official Intelligence, London, various years

NEWSPAPERS

The British Columbia Mining Record, Victoria, B.C.
The Canadian Gazette, London
The Canadian Mining and Mechanical Review, Ottawa
The Canadian Mining Journal, Toronto
The Economist, London
The Monetary Times, Toronto
The Statist, London

GOVERNMENT SOURCES

Annual Reports on the Mineral Production of Canada During the Calendar Year, Department of Mines, Ottawa, various years
'Chronological Record of Canadian Mining Events, 1604–1943,' see above, 1944. 'Historical Summary of Canada's Mineral Production,' see above, 1944.
'Annual Reports of the Department of the Interior,' Department of the Interior, *Sessional Papers*, Ottawa, various years
'Annual Reports of the Department of Marine and Fisheries,' Department of Marine and Fisheries, *Sessional Papers*, Ottawa, various years
'Annual Report of the Minister of Mines for the Year,' *Sessional Papers of the Province of British Columbia*, Victoria, B.C., various years
'Annual Reports of the Department of Trade and Commerce,' Department of Trade and Commerce, *Sessional Papers*, Ottawa, various years
BOSTOCK, H.S., *Yukon Territory, Selected Field Reports of the Geological Survey of Canada*, 1898 to 1933, Geological Survey of Canada, Memoir 284, Ottawa, 1957
BRECHER, I. and REISMAN, S.S., *Canada-United States Economic Relations*, Royal Commission on Canada's Economic Prospects, Ottawa, 1957
British and Foreign Direct Investment in Canada and Canadian Direct Investments Abroad, 1936, Department of Trade and Commerce, Ottawa, 1938
'British Columbia Fishery Commission Report, 1892,' Department of Marine and Fisheries, *Sessional Papers*, No. 10C, Ottawa, 1893
British Columbia, *The Mineral Province of Canada, 1902*, Provincial Bureau of Mines, Victoria, B.C., 1902
British Columbia, The Mineral Province of Canada, 1905, Provincial Bureau of Mines, Victoria, B.C., 1905

The Canada Year Book, Ottawa, various issues

Canada as a Field for British Branch Industries, Department of Trade and Commerce, Ottawa, 1922

Canada's Fertile Northland, Evidence Heard Before a Select Committee of the Senate of Canada, ed. E.J. Chambers, Department of the Interior, Ottawa, 1908

Canada's International Investment Position, 1926–1954, Dominion Bureau of Statistics, Ottawa, 1954

The Canadian Balance of International Payments, A Study of Methods and Results, Dominion Bureau of Statistics, Ottawa, 1939

The Canadian Balance of International Payments in the Post-War Years, 1946–1952, Dominion Bureau of Statistics, Ottawa, 1953

Dominions Royal Commission, Final Report (reprint of Cd. 8462), London, 1918

Economic Minerals and Mining Industries of Canada, Department of Mines, Ottawa, 1913

'Evidence on the Export Cattle Trade of Canada,' Department of Marine and Fisheries, *Sessional Papers*, No. 78, Ottawa, 1891

LONG, J., *Canadian Agriculture: A Report by Prof. James Long*, Department of the Interior, London, 1894

The Nickel Industry, Department of Mines, Ottawa, 1913

Preliminary Reports on the Mineral Production of Canada during the Calendar Year, Department of Mines, Ottawa, various years

The Postal Census of Manufacturers, 1916, Dominion Bureau of Statistics, Ottawa, 1917

The Production of Copper, Gold, Lead, Nickel, Silver, Zinc, and Other Metals in Canada during the Calendar Year, Department of Mines, Ottawa, various years

The Production of Coal and Coke in Canada during the Calendar Year, Department of Mines, Ottawa, various years

'Report of J.B. Tyrell,' *Yukon Territory, Selected Field Reports of the Geological Survey of Canada, 1898–1933*, ed. H.S. Bostock, Geological Survey of Canada, Memoir 284, Ottawa, 1957

'Report of the Commission ...' *Commission to Inquire into Treadgold and Other Concessions in the Yukon Territory, Sessional Papers*, No. 142, Ottawa, 1904

Report of the Royal Commission on the Mineral Resources of Ontario, Legislative Assembly of Ontario, Toronto, 1890

Report of the Royal Ontario Nickel Commission, Royal Ontario Nickel Commission, Legislative Assembly of Ontario, Toronto, 1917

Report on the Mining and Metallurgical Industries of Canada, 1907–8, Department of Mines, Ottawa, 1908
Statistical Abstracts for the United Kingdom, London, various years
The Statistical Year-Book of Canada, Department of Agriculture, Ottawa, various years
Urban and Rural Development, Report of a Conference held at Winnipeg, May 28th–30th, 1917, Commission of Conservation, Ottawa, 1917
Wallace, R., *Special Report on the Agricultural Resources of Canada*, Department of the Interior, London 1894
The Yukon Territory, Its History and Resources, Department of Mines, Ottawa, 1909

BOOKS

AITKEN, H.G.J. et al. *The American economic impact on Canada*, Durham, N.C., 1961
– *American capital and Canadian resources*, Cambridge, Mass., 1961
ANDERSON, I.A. *Internal migration in Canada, 1921–1961*, Staff Study no. 13, Economic Council of Canada, Ottawa, 1966
BARKER, T.C. *Pilkington Brothers and the glass industry*, London, 1960
BLOOMFIELD, A.I. *Short-term capital movements under the pre-1914 gold standard*, Princeton Studies in International Finance No. 11, Princeton, N.J., 1963
– *Patterns of fluctuations in international investment before 1914*, Princeton Studies in International Finance No. 21, Princeton, N.J., 1968
BOAM, H.J. *British Columbia, its history, people, commerce, industries and resources*, London, 1912
BRADLEY, A.G. *Canada in the twentieth century*, London, 1905
BRECHER, I. *Capital flows between Canada and the United States*, Montreal, 1963
BRECKENRIDGE, R.M. *The Canadian banking system, 1817–1890*, New York, 1895
n.a. *British Columbia as a field for emigration and investment*, Victoria, B.C., 1891
– *British Columbia, its present resources and future possibilities*, Victoria, B.C., 1893
BRITNELL, G.E. *The wheat economy*, Toronto, 1939

BUCKLEY, K.A.H. *Capital formation in Canada, 1896–1930*, Toronto, 1955, and 'Capital formation in Canada,' in *Problems in Capital Formation*, N.B.E.R., Princeton, N.J., 1957

BURLEY, K.H. *The development of Canada's staples, 1867–1939*, Toronto, 1970

BURNS, A.F. and MITCHELL, W.C. *Measuring business cycles*, New York, 1946

BURTON, H. and CORNER, D.C. *Investment and unit trusts in Britain and America*, London, 1968

Business men at home and abroad: 1912–1913, ed. H.H. Bassett, London, 1912

CAIRNCROSS, A.K. *Home and foreign investment, 1870–1913*, Cambridge, 1953

CAVES, R. and HOLTON, R.H. *The Canadian economy, prospect and retrospect*, Cambridge, Mass., 1959

CLAPHAM, J.H. *An economic history of modern Britain*, Vol. III, Cambridge, 1938

CONWAY, T. and ATWOOD, A.W. *Investment and speculation*, ed. F.W. Field, New York, 1914

COOKE, C.A. *Corporation, trust and company, an essay in legal history*, Manchester, 1950

CREAMER, D., DOBROVOLSKY, S.P., and BORNSTEIN, I. *Capital in manufacturing and mining*, N.B.E.R., Princeton, N.J., 1960

DALES, J.H. *Hydroelectricity and industrial development, Quebec, 1898–1940*, Cambridge, Mass., 1957

DUNNING, J.H. *American investment in British manufacturing industry*, London, 1958

– *The role of American investment in the British economy*, London, 1969

EASTERBROOK, W.T. *Farm credit in Canada*, Toronto, 1938

EASTERBROOK, W.T. and AITKEN, H.G.J. *Canadian economic history*, Toronto, 1963

FIELD, F.W. *Capital investments in Canada*, Toronto, 1911

– *Capital investments in Canada*, Toronto, 1914

FIRESTONE, O.J. *Canada's economic development, 1867–1953*, Income and Wealth Series, VII, London, 1958

FRANKEL, S.H. *Investment and the return to equity capital in the South African gold mining industry, 1887–1965*, Oxford, 1967

– *Gold and international equity investment*, London, 1969

GALBRAITH, J.S. *The Hudson's Bay Company as an imperial factor, 1821–1869*, Los Angeles, 1957

GIBBON, J.M. 'The Scot in Canada' (*Aberdeen Daily Journal*), Aberdeen 1907

HILTON, G.W. and DUE, J.F. *The electric interurban railways in America*, Stanford, 1960

HOBSON, C.K. *The export of capital*, London, 1914

HUNT, B.C. *The development of the business corporation in England, 1800–1867*, Cambridge, Mass., 1936

IMLAH, A.H. *Economic elements in the Pax Britannica*, Cambridge, Mass., 1958

JACKSON, W.T. *The enterprising Scot, investors in the American west after 1873*, Edinburgh, 1968

KINDLEBERGER, C.P. *International economics*, Homewood, Ill., 1963

LAVINGTON, F. *The English capital market*, London, 1921

LAYTON, C. *Trans-Atlantic investment*, Boulogne-Sur-Seine, France, 1967

LEVITT, K. *Silent surrender, the multinational corporation in Canada*, Toronto, 1970

LEWIS, C. *America's stake in international investments* (The Brookings Institution), Washington, 1938

LOWER, A.R.M. and INNIS, H.A. *Settlement and the forest and mining frontiers* (Canadian Frontiers of Settlement, Vol. IX), Toronto, 1936

MACDONALD, N. *Canada, immigration and colonization 1841–1903*, Aberdeen, 1966

McINNIS, E. *Canada, a political and social history*, Rev. ed., Toronto, 1964

McPHEE, C.C. *Commercial Canada*, Ottawa, 1904

MAIN, W.O. *The Canadian nickel industry*, Toronto, 1955

MARSHALL, H., SOUTHARD, F.A., and TAYLOR, K.W. *Canadian-American industry*, New Haven, Conn., 1936

MEIER, G.M. *Leading issues in development economics*, New York, 1964

MIKESELL, R.F. *Foreign investments in Latin America* (Pan American Union), Washington, 1955

MITCHELL, B.R. and DEANE, P. *Abstract of British historical statistics*, Cambridge, 1962

MOORE, S.E. *The American influence in Canadian mining*, Toronto, 1941

MORGAN, E.V. and THOMAS, W.A. *The stock exchange: its history and functions*, London, 1962

MORTON, A.S. and MARTIN, C. *The history of prairie settlement and 'Dominion Lands' policy*, Toronto, 1938

MURCHIE, R.W. et al. *Agricultural progress on the prairie frontier* (Canadian Frontiers of Settlement, Vol. V), Toronto, 1936

The problem of international investment, 1937. A Report by a Study Group of Members of the Royal Institute of International Affairs, reprinted, London, 1965

The Province of Alberta, an official handbook, ed. W.T. Finlay, Edmonton, 1907

PEARCE, W.M. *The Matador Land and Cattle Company*, Norman, Okla, 1964

RAMACHANDRAN, N. *Foreign plantation investment in Ceylon, 1889-1958*, Ceylon, 1963

REDDAWAY, W.B. et al. *Effects of U.K. direct investment overseas: An Interim Report* (University of Cambridge, Department of Applied Economics, Occasional Paper 12), Cambridge, 1967

- *Effects of U.K. direct investment overseas: a final report* (University of Cambridge, Department of Applied Economics, Occasional Paper 15), Cambridge, 1968

'Report of the Ontario Mining Institute,' reprinted in *The Canadian Mining and Mechanical Review*, 1894

RIPPY, J.F. *British investments in Latin America*, Hamden, Conn. 1959

ROUSSEAUX, P. *Les mouvements de fonds de l'economie anglaise, 1800-1913*, Louvain, France, 1938

SAUL, S.B. *Studies in British overseas trade, 1870-1914*, Liverpool, 1960

SCHMITTHOFF, C. and CURRY, T.P.E. *Palmer's company law*, 20th ed., London, 1959

'Silver and Gold,' *Cobalt Daily Nugget*, Cobalt, Ont., 1916

SPEIGAL, M. *Statistics*, New York, 1961

SINGH, A. and WHITTINGTON, G. *Growth, profitability and valuation*, University of Cambridge, Department of Applied Economics, Occasional Paper 7, Cambridge, 1968

SPENCE, C.C. *British investments and the mining frontier*, Ithaca, N.Y., 1958

STOVEL, J.A. *Canada in the world economy*, Cambridge, Mass., 1959

STURNEY, A.C. *The story of Mond nickel* (privately printed), London, 1961

Studies in Scottish business history, ed. P.L. Payne, London, 1967

TAYLOR, K.W. and MITCHELL, H. *Statistical contributions to Canadian economic history*, 2 vols., Toronto, 1931

THOMAS, R. *Migration and economic growth*, Cambridge, 1972

United Nations, *External financing in Latin America*, Department of Economic and Social Affairs, New York, 1965

URQUHART, M.C. and BUCKLEY, K.A.H. *Historical statistics of Canada*, Toronto, 1963

VINER, J. *Canada's balance of international indebtedness, 1900-1913*, Cambridge, Mass., 1924

WEINBURG, M.A. *Take-overs and amalgamations*, London, 1963

WILKINS, M. *The emergence of multinational enterprise: American business abroad from the Colonial Crate 1914*, Cambridge, Mass., 1970

– *The maturing of multinational enterprise: American business abroad from 1914 to 1970*, Cambridge, Mass., 1974

WILLIAMSON, J.G. *American growth and the balance of payments, 1820-1913*, Durham, N.C., 1964

Yukon Goldfields (A report to the shareholders of Yukon Goldfields, Ltd.): dated 19 Dec. 1899

ARTICLES

ABRAMOVITZ, M. 'The nature and significance of Kuznets Cycles,' *Economic Development and Cultural Change*, 9, no. 3 (1961), 225-48

ALDCROFT, D. 'The entrepreneur and the British economy, 1870-1914' reprinted in *The British economy, 1870-1914*, eds. D. Aldcroft and H. Richardson (London, 1969), pp. 141-67

ARKELL, H.S. 'The cattle industry' in *Twentieth century impressions of Canada*, London, 1914

BECKHART, B.H. 'Fewer and larger banks,' in *Money and banking*, ed. E.P. Neufeld (Toronto, 1964), pp. 196-205

BERTRAM, G. 'Economic growth in Canadian industry, 1870-1915: the staple model and the take-off hypothesis,' *Canadian Journal of Economics and Political Science*, 29, no. 2 (1963), 159-84

BICHA, K.D. 'The plains farmer and the prairie province frontier, 1897-1914,' *Journal of Economic History*, 25, no. 2 (1965), 263-70

BLYTH, C.D. and CARBY, E.B. 'Non-resident ownership of Canadian industry,' *Canadian Journal of Economics and Political Science*, 22, no. 4 (1956), 449-60

BOND, D.E. 'The merger movement in Canadian banking, 1900-1914,' Unpublished paper, the University of British Columbia, 1969

BRAYER, H.O. 'The influence of British capital on the western range-cattle industry,' *Journal of Economic History*, 9, suppl. (1949), 85-98

BRILL, D.H. 'Financing capital formation,' *Problems of capital formation* (Studies in Income and Wealth, Vol. 19, N.B.E.R.), Princeton, N.J. (1957), pp. 147-200

BUCKLEY, K.A.H. 'The role of staple industries in Canada's economic development,' *Journal of Economic History*, 8, no. 4 (1958), 439-50

- 'Urban building and real estate fluctuations in Canada,' *Canadian Journal of Economics and Political Science*, 8, no. 1 (1952), 41-62

CAIRNCROSS, A.K. 'Investment in Canada, 1900-1913,' reprinted in *The export of capital from Britain, 1870-1914*, ed. A.R. Hall (London, 1968), pp. 153-86

CHAMBERS, E.D. 'Late nineteenth century business cycles in Canada,' *Canadian Journal of Economics and Political Science*, 30, no 3 (1964), 391-412

FEINSTEIN, C.H. 'Income and investment in the United Kingdom, 1856-1914,' *Economic Journal*, 71 (June 1961), 367-85

FIRESTONE, O.J. 'Canada's external trade and net foreign balance, 1851-1900,' in *Trends in the American economy in the nineteenth century*, Studies in Income and Wealth, Vol. 24, N.B.E.R. (Princeton, N.J., 1960), pp. 757-71

FORD, A.G. 'Notes on the working of the gold standard before 1914,' *Oxford Economic Papers*, II (1960), 52-76

- 'The transfer of British foreign lending, 1870-1913,' *Economic History Review*, Second Series, 11, no. 2 (1958), 302-8

HARLEY, C.K. 'Skilled labour and the choice in Edwardian industry,' *Explorations in Economic History*, 11, no. 4 (1974), 391-414

HARTLAND, P. 'Factors in economic growth in Canada,' *Journal of Economic History*, 15, no. 1 (1955), 13-22

- 'Canadian balance of payments since 1868,' in *Trends in the American economy in the nineteenth century*, Studies in Income and Wealth, Vol. 24, N.B.E.R. (Princeton, N.J., 1960), pp. 717-55 and 'Comments'

HAY, K.A.'Money in post-confederation Canada,' *Journal of Political Economy* (June 1967), 263-71

IMLAH, A.H. 'British balance of payments and export of capital, 1816-1913,' *Economic History Review*, Second Series, 5, no. 2 (1952), 208-39

INGRAM, J.C. 'Growth and capacity in Canada's balance of payments,' *American Economic Review*, 127, no. 1 (1957), 93-104

INNIS, H.A. 'The Canadian mining industry,' in *Essays in Canadian Economic History*, ed. M.Q. Innis (Toronto, 1962), pp. 309-20

KNOX, F.A. 'Excursus, Canadian capital movements and the Canadian balance of payments, 1900-1934,' in Marshall, H. et al., *Canadian-American industry* (New Haven, Conn., 1936), pp. 296-324

KUZNETS, S. 'Long-term trends in capital formation proportions,' *Economic Development and Cultural Change*, 9, no. 4, Part II (1961), 1-124

LEWIS, W.A. and O'LEARY, P.J. 'Secular swings in production and trade cycles, 1870-1913,' *Manchester School* (1955), 113-46

McCLOSKEY, D.N. 'Did Victorian Britain fail?' *Economic History Review*, Second Series, 33, no. 3 (1970), 446-59

McCLOSKEY, D.N. and SANDBERG, L.G. 'From damnation to redemption: judgments on the late Victorian entrepreneur,' *Explorations in Economic History*, 9, no. 1 (1971), 89-108

MACDONALD, N. 'Seattle, Vancouver, and the Klondyke,' *Canadian Historical Review*, 49 (Sept. 1968), 234-46

MacDOUGALL, G.A.D. 'The benefits and costs of private investment from abroad: a theoretical approach,' reprinted in *International Trade*, ed. J. Bhagwati (Middlesex, 1969), pp. 341-69

MARTIN, K. 'Capital movements, the terms of trade and the balance of payments,' *Bulletin of the Oxford University Institute of Statistics*, 11, no. 11 (1949), 357-66

MEIER, G.M. 'Economic development and the transfer mechanism in Canada,' *Canadian Journal of Economics and Political Science*, 19, no. 1 (1953), 1-19

MORSE, C. 'Potentials and hazards of direct international investment in raw materials,' in *Natural resources and international development*, ed. M. Clawson (Baltimore, 1964), 367-414

PAZOS, F. 'The role of international movements of private capital in promoting development,' in *Capital movements and economic development*, ed. J.H. Adler (London, 1967), pp. 186-208

PENNER, R.S. 'The benefits of foreign investment in Canada, 1950 to 1956,' *Canadian Journal of Economics and Political Science*, 32, no. 2 (1966), 172-83

PENTLAND, H.C. 'The role of capital in Canadian economic development before 1875,' *Canadian Journal of Economics and Political Science*, 16, no. 4 (1950), 457-74

PREST, A.R. and TURVEY, R. 'Cost-benefit analysis: a survey,' in *Surveys of economic theory*, Vol. III (A.E.A. and R.E.S.) (London, 1968), pp. 155-207

SAFARIAN, A.E. 'The exports of American owned enterprises in Canada,' *A.E.R. Papers and Proceedings* (1964), pp. 449-58 and discussion

SCAPERLANDA, A.E. and MAUER, L.J. 'The determinants of U.S. direct investment in the E.E.C.,' *American Economic Review*, 59, no. 4 (1969), 558-68

SCOTT, A. 'The development of the extractive industries,' *Canadian Journal of Economics and Political Science*, 27, no. 1 (1962), 70-87

SIMON, M. 'The pattern of new British portfolio investment, 1865-1914,' in *Capital movements and economic development*, ed. J.H. Adler (London, 1967), pp. 33-60, and comments

- 'New British investments in Canada, 1865-1914,' *Canadian Journal of Economics*, 3, no. 2 (1970), 238-54

STONE, I. 'British long-term investment in Latin America, 1865-1913,' *Business History Review*, 42, no. 3 (1968), 311-39

STOPFORD, J.M. 'The origins of British-based multinational manufacturing enterprises,' *Business History Review*, 48, no. 3 (1974), 303-35

THOMAS, B. 'The historical record of international capital movements to 1913,' in *Capital movements and economic development*, ed. J.H. Adler (London, 1967), pp. 3-32

VON TUNZELMAN, G.N. 'The new economic history: an econometric appraisal,' reprinted in *The new economic history*, ed. R.L. Andreano (New York, 1970), pp. 151-75

YOUNG, J.H. 'Comparative economic development: Canada and the United States,' *American Economic Review*, 45, no. 1 (1955), 80-93

Index